Trout Reflections

Also by the author:

The Year of the Turtle: A Natural History

Written and
Illustrated by

David M. Carroll

Trout Reflections

A Natural
History of the
Trout and Its World

ST. MARTIN'S PRESS   •   NEW YORK

The author would like to credit Penguin USA for the quotation from William Butler Yeats's poem, "Song of the Wandering Aengus," published in The Celtic Twilight. Grateful acknowledgment is given to Annie Dillard and to HarperCollins for permission to quote from Teaching a Stone to Talk, as it is to Simon & Schuster for permission to quote Thomas McGuane from Season of the Angler, edited by David Seybold.

ISBN 0-312-09464-7

Jacket and text designed by Jaye Zimet

PRINTED IN HONG KONG
FIRST EDITION: APRIL 1993

10 9 8 7 6 5 4 3 2 1

For My Mother
and for Bill and DeDe Miller

CONTENTS

CHAPTER FOUR

Solstice: Time of Low Water

CHAPTER FIVE

Turning Leaves and Early Dark

CHAPTER SIX

The Closing Over: Return to Silence

ACKNOWLEDGMENTS

Paul Bofinger, a trout man in every best sense of the word, and one who has done so much for the preservation of wild places, provided inspirational enthusiasm for this project and granted me generous, long-term access to his wonderful library. The focus and insights of my wife, Laurette, were of sustained and immeasurable help in the development of this book. Brian Butler, who possesses a keen scientific and intuitive knowledge of wild waterways, was a source of stimulating communication, and he aided me tremendously in tracking down the trout literature. I am thankful for the support and encouragement I received from Hank and Lois Aplington. Michael Sagalyn's appreciation for my writing and art played a key role in the realization of this book, as did the enduring efforts of my agents, Meredith Bernstein and Elizabeth Cavanaugh. I thank my editor, Barbara Anderson, for her heartening response to this work, and for great service in editing a lengthy and complex manuscript. Duncan McInnes of the New Hampshire Department of Fish and Game offered helpful access to that agency's resources, and Jim Piper and the good people at the New Hampton hatchery assisted me in obtaining glimpses into the elusive world of wild brook trout. I thank the Fred W. Courser family and the Bates families, and other landholders public and private, who helped make possible access to unspoiled streams. I am deeply grateful to the researchers, conservationists, and anglers whose devoted, ongoing efforts help preserve the perilously diminishing natural world of the trout.

Trout Reflections

World of Silence:
Ice and Snow

Blue mist at sundown. • Birds' cries stir the stream water. • Follow the stream's turn into some depth— • Such quietude: no end.

—P'ei Ti

Between Snows: 5 January

Between snows in early January I walk out onto the mantle of ice and snow that covers the meadow pond. I can walk on water now, walk over the world of the trout. The sky has gone as gray as the ice where wind-sweep has kept it clear of snow. Most of the small pond is a pure white plain, against which are set the black and straw-gold scripts of emergent grass, rush, sedge, and shrub; fine-lined writing on a white ground. Ice shows in tracings and swirls around the stalks and fallen straps of cattail leaves along the pond's border. These cattails are like flameless torches loosening a downy, brown-white smoke of seed across the snow. I move on through other dried plants above the ice: soft rush, its pointed sienna shafts and delicate flower sprays as perfect in form in winter as they were in their green growth of summer; and woolly-looking sedges and tall bulrushes.

The brook that flows from this pond is lively beneath the sleeping land-scape. Its song, encased in crystal, is muted and seems to come from a distance, as do all the songs of winter. This elemental water,

Water running over stones

rushing or trickling through time and the seasons, sliding over stone, regathering in a riffled race over gravel, slowing and drifting through alder and willow lowlands, meandering among wet meadows, tracing its vital course through the landscape, moves ever downstream, until it becomes cloudborne and returns to its source in the rains and snows of future seasons. The brook carves the land that cradles it, and shapes and arranges the stones that define the route it takes. Here in this vein of quickened silver, where water braids light and weaves together sun and shadow, trout take form and disappear.

Whether riding the spring flood in water more wild than any skyscape, or suspended in still, dark pools at the time of low water, or jousting and coupling in clear, chill spawning riffles, in motion or in stillness, trout arrange themselves perfectly in the medium of their lives. They know the January snowlight, the countless grays of thaw, summer's glaring bronze, and autumn's undulating blaze. Alert to wingshadows, searching banded stones for patterned insects, mindful of every speck or spreading ring of darkness on the quivering ceiling of their world, with senses and intelligence trout read, interpret, and define each message and moment. One can see an imagined trout, or imagine a seen one. They seem to be an idea that comes and goes in the water's restless mind. Trout are water and themselves, they are the sun-gold in the stream. They are wavering bars of light, ever-changing in the water, and the rippled darks and near-darks of shadows, fountain moss, sunken bark, and stone.

Trout on Snow: 15 January

At midday I turn from the white avenue of an old railroad bed and pass through a screen of upland woods, to the crest of one of the steepest slopes along Blackwater Brook. Digging my feet sideways into the soft snow and placing them one below the other while holding onto whips of ironwood sprouts, I ease my way down the embankment toward a strip of black water.

January fishing. On milder days the bits of open water along this wild, untrafficked brook offer the promise of trout. Upon reaching a narrow level densely grown with alders, I cave through several layers thinner than glass, then plant my feet on solid shelvings of ice. The tinkling of scattered ice dies away, and the restless shouldering of water against glacial banks becomes the only sound along the snow-silenced landscape. Lodged among the bordering alders I prepare to fish deep, entrusting the current just beyond my boot-tips to carry my offerings to the noses of any trout who may be holding in the pool just below.

This is one of the places to which I come throughout the year, and fish once a season. Never certain how it goes with the speckled natives of this brook, I take the daily limit as my annual limit: five trout. The water is 0°C, 32°F, right at freezing no matter how it is measured. It is richly aerated in any case, and there is an insulating factor in the snow-drifted mantle of ice that has bridged nearly the entire extent of the brook. I suspect groundwater may enter this pool at some point, as brook trout retreat here in the heat and drought of summer. If seeps or a spring enter, their constant 45°–50°F temperature range, which cools in summer, would warm the water some in

winter. But it simply may be that depth and abundant cover alone make this a trout-hold through the year. In water this close to becoming transformed into solid ice, trout do feed, but could go four months without eating. Winter indifference will therefore factor in whatever I offer any ice-water fish.

This is one of the few sections of the miles of brooks I traverse and sometimes fish in which a minnow imitation might find success. In recent years I have caught and released a couple of brook trout between fourteen and fifteen inches fork length, standout occasions each. I have seen shadow shapes and wakes in the water during warmer times of the year, and flashes of bronze in the darkened, brandywine pools of autumn—instants intimating that I have yet to see clearly the largest of the trout that dwell in them. On several occasions, remembered more vividly than those of trout caught, my line has held so briefly and telegraphed back to me the weight and pull, the electric surging of resisting life that surely must have been the take of a brook trout of a length I have never had the chance to calculate. I do not fish the fabled Nipigon of former brook-trout glory; the black-and-silver runs of water I frequent are not tributary to the legendary Broadback and Mistassini watersheds of scrub-pine forests far to the north. But these streams constitute a native world with native trout, and as they are left remarkably to themselves for now in a time of increasingly hounded natural habitat, somewhere in the deeper riffles, thicket-shrouded pools, and black undercuts of impassable banks, some of the bejeweled and speckled trout must achieve their full potential age and size.

I take to these untouched brooks to keep appointments with the seasons, and sometimes to fish. There is something that draws me here, something in the watching and the wading, the "being here" that links me to another kind of native, that race of my own species, the Native Americans, who lived here for thousands of years without taking a single thread of running water from the enormous tapestry of the wild landscape. Another race, the stream-changers and river-takers of the past few hundred years, seems never to have possessed such a sensibility. This American land and its natives, from human to trout, have suffered and declined continually since their arrival.

The water's rippling, the January sun on the speckled, maroon-gray bark of the alders, and a twitch of nearly invisible line in my fingertips bring my focus back to the brook running by me. An incomplete angler, I have probably hooked more fish in an unconscious state than when at my most alert. Racing or as unmoving as glass, water mesmerizes. A brisk slip of line from my hand brings me sharply back to thoughts of trout. The line goes slack…then there is a pull, or is it a steady weight? Working the distances of a brook, one can confuse stone and fish. Now something signals back along the line, and it is alive. After all these years, how can the pulling of a fish set the heart to pounding? Excitement equals youth: perhaps we go after trout to rediscover that we

are yet this alive. I set, too sharply it seems, then let the line go slack, a tendency in times of uncertainty. I do not fish enough to have had right action become instinct, and intermittent winter layoffs diminish knowledge and reactions. There are so many variables that anglers, from the luck-dependent to the most complete, never want for challenges, or new experiences. For those who fish, the quest is endless, and will be so as long as trout waters flow.

In ice-water by ice-light, a fish works strongly against my efforts to turn him. My anxiety quickens as I gain a feel of the impressive weight, even a sense of the will of what must be one of this brook's largest trout. This fish is as cold as the water, but vibrantly alive and forceful, and clearly has no desire to be drawn forth into the January sunlight. "Let me see this trout," I ask of the water; but the ever-sliding surface with its mask of sky and clouds flows on, revealing nothing. Beneath the immutable ice, the fish fights on. I cannot be wrong about the feel: this is a trout, and in this brook it can only be a native brook trout. Our resolute tug-of-war goes on. I am driven by a vision of a great speckled fish, flame-finned and crimson-splashed; he is driven to keep his life. I have only a shadowy notion of the trout I feel but cannot see, but this vague image must be a complete picture compared to any idea he can have of the force that turns him in the water he has always pierced so freely, the unseen predator that seems intent on tearing him from his stream. The trout breaks free. This is how it is: in the pound-

ing of the heart, the carelessness of feet made awkward by excitement at the water's edge, the fears of snags and tangles, the confusion of thought and instinct, the line goes slack. And in that slackening, the heart empties for a moment. I am on both knees in snow and ice, right at the black edge of the racing stream, where among my whirling thoughts I had been trying to remember what part of the run lay beneath me, and to decide whether entering the icy brook would help my cause. Academic now, all these thoughts and strategies. Those seconds of playing the fish seem to have lasted forever, the kind of seconds that can balance out hours of working an empty line. My feelings begin to level. The trout will recover quickly, and has a season to forget this encounter. He did not require me to cut him free. I know that a remarkable fish has sped to deepest cover, and remains in the brook's keeping. Whatever elements of the mysteries and fascinations of natural history, of instincts, esthetics, or solitude combine in the fishing, however one comes to terms with the killing or releasing, there is always the compelling hold, the dream of the big fish. The actual and symbolic draw of the great fish held in secret by the water is not dependent upon the great salt sea or even a moody expanse of river; it can come among the alders lining a narrow, remnant brook from which the wildness has not been taken. We fish the waters for trout, but in the end, it is we who are caught by the waters.

With the unsolicited assistance of a knife of ice, I have practiced the catch-and-release technique recommended for ice-fishing, when one has a sort of reverse fisherman's luck and hooks, during a must-release season, a salmon instead of a lake or rainbow trout that might be kept. Even if a fish is not lifted from the frigid water, handling it in order to remove a hook is worse than simply cutting the line and setting it free. Even deeply hooked fish have a survival rate of up to 90 percent when released in this manner. Any handling increases mortality. The use of a smaller hook, such as a size 8, enhances a fish's chances for surviving. The great trout held by my line for this brief time has gone not only untouched by human hands, but unseen by human eyes. I look into the black water, where slivers of ice begin to link one to another as the frozen shelving along the brook rebuilds its broken edge.

With the help of spring alders, I rise to my feet. My knees are stiff, and the getting-up is slow, but the day is mild and I have not gotten wet; there is no need to give up fishing. I am certain that more than one trout is overwintering in this pool, and if one has been moved to feed, perhaps another will. I repeat the tactics that hooked the fish that got away, though it is strange how the adrenaline-laced moments of hooking and playing a trout can obscure the details one vows to remember: how deep the water, swift the flow, just how close to a bank or other obstruction, or what type of open water; what fly, lure or bait and how presented...even the time of day and season can blur. Many settings, many images of trout in their world, have become indelibly recorded in my mind; especially sightings of native trout, which are more hard-won than the hookings. Though I never saw this fish, and in time will forget the mechanical angling aspects of the experience, the feel of the trout and of my moments with him along this brook will travel back up the steep slope with me, and live with me.

From the alder's enclosure I work the steady flow of water and test the depths beneath the ice. In time, a trout message comes back. I tense for an instant, but immediately realize that this cannot be the fish I lost. Still, the dogged downward pull is forceful, and this one is also lively. I have not seen a native brook trout close at hand since the woodbine blazed in dead trees along this stream last autumn. I work him to the surface, and guide this thrashing fish into the slush off the borders of the solid shelf. He makes a sudden thrust and launches himself onto snow, out of water, lying still for an instant, brilliant against the stunning whiteness. I am eager to return him to the stream, to the pool from which he has been so reluctantly summoned. I strain to divide the fleeting time in half and take in the scene before me, with its swirlings of black water against the silver-grays of the ice, the shimmering fish on blinding snow, the maze of scarlet dogwood branches all around. The green-gold brook trout, speckled with cadmium yellow and flecked with crimson, swims into drifted powder. He has never known his ambient element in this crystalline form. His belly,

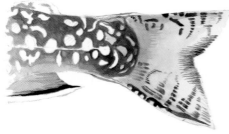

with its flaring of orange-gold and red, seems to burn against the snow. Somehow, this dazzling fish does not look out of place in his moment on snow. The brilliant reds of his flared fins hark back to the origins of one of his names: "char," or "charr," which derives from the Gaelic language, from an Old Irish word for blood red. His graceful, beautifully proportioned length is patterned with spots, and flecks of pale lemon and deep orange-gold, which glow out from their encircling overlay of deep umber-green. These stippled lights radiating out from a dark ground are one of the identifying characteristics that mark the brook trout as a char, brother to the arctic char of boreal rivers and seas. This patterning is reversed in brown trout, as it is in rainbow and the other western trout, all of which feature scatterings of black spots on the light, glowing backgrounds of their shimmering sides. This trout's fin-edges are as white as the snow against which they disappear, another marking that reflects his kinship with the arctic char.

Char, trout, salmon, grayling…these salmonids are all denizens of cold waters. Born of glaciers, they seem to have taken their colors from sunlight glinting on ice-fractures, from sunset and twilight glows across fields of ice; they are radiant and light-filled, as intensely spectral as the rainbows that sunlight throws off meltwater, as softly glowing as tinted ribbons pulsed into the night sky by the northern lights.

Colors and patterns take form and

9

movement as the hooked trout thrusts against the snow and leaps back into the water. The vermiculations of his back become an aspect of the brook that swirls around him. My hands are agonized the moment I plunge them into the water to cut the restraining leader and free this bright char. I feel as though I set a jewel back into its rightful place in the silver crown of the brook. At a temperature of 32°F this water would draw the life from me in seconds, but this glacier-child is in his element. Salmonids originated in the northern hemisphere, and although their fossil record is sparse and disjointed, it is believed that they appeared about one hundred million years ago, rather recently by fish standards. Over the course of their history they have been driven southward by the advance of glaciers, and pursued them back to the north in periods of global warming, following in the very meltwater steps of retreating mountains of ice. The arctic char lives farther north than any other freshwater fish; this and other salmonid species and their many strains and races keep to chill waters even south of the regions of frozen winters, holding out in icy bowls and runs of snowmelt high in the tops of mountains, or close to frigid groundwater seeps and springs. Where there is cold, pure, richly oxygenated water, there can be trout. And so there are gleaming trout native to the desert country of the southwestern United States, and even in Mexico, where such species as the apache, gila, and Mexican golden trout live high above the burning sands in headwater mountain streams at altitudes ranging from 6,000 to 8,000 feet.

The trout I glimpsed against snow in the midwinter sun is gone in his deep pool. He is native to this water and knows its ways. At about eleven inches, he has made it through two previous winters, and is likely to survive the one at hand. This wild brook is never stocked and its trout are its own. Rich in varied habitat, this waterway's precious diversity provides niches for different age classes, individuals, and aggregates of overwintering trout. Those in their first winter would have a tendency to take to shallower, slower water than the older, larger trout. The largest, such as the one I felt

*Arctic char (*Salvelinus alpinus*)*

on my line today, would be likely to hold in the deepest pools. Some of the natives of the lowest reaches of this brook may migrate downstream and pass the time of ice and snow in deep pools in the river. From stream to stream, the sites chosen for over-wintering may be quite different, depending on habitat available and the water's flow and freeze characteristics. In some situations even larger trout will spend the winter in shallow braids of water entering the main flow, if the current is slow enough in the braid, and there is dense cover. There is cer-tainly dense cover available along this brook, where long reaches are lined with crisscrossing, intergrown branches of silky dogwood and alder. Many entire stream sec-tions are completely enclosed by this and other riparian growth, from the water sur-face to a height of eight to ten feet. There are few runs of open water along the brooks I frequent. This realm of the brook trout, which I can not only look into, but also physically enter from thaw until freeze, is almost completely separated from me now. I am divided from these beautiful, speckled swimmers by long, silent corridors of snow-covered ice, beneath which water slides as silently as the shadows that sweep across them. This thick, horizontal screen is the trout's winter ceiling, my winter floor.

February Brooks: 7 February

From my vantage point atop the beaver dam, I look back across the blanketed pond, beyond its tawny stands of sedge and cattail, and the bordering sweeps of reed canary grass to the distinct shrub-rows that mark its two inlets. One is a narrow, seasonal brook with headwaters in the seep-springs in the hills above the meadow. Its final level run into the pond is lined almost entirely with pussy willows and occasional out-growths of alder and silky willow. The deep-er, broader inlet brook wanders over level ground, yet keeps a slow, steady current in all but the driest times, as it is fed by drainages from steep hills on either side, and has a permanent pond at its source. Dense alder and silky dogwood thickets border this brook, which is accented by the only tall tree in the meadow landscape, a twisting, thirty-foot upreach of the several trunks of a peachleaf willow. The growth along both of these brooks encloses them with canopies of leaves in summer, branches in winter. Below me the outlet cuts through reed-grass and sedge turf with enough tur-bulence to keep some open water even in January, as it races to join the main stream and, eventually, the river. Trout are here, somewhere within this ice-bridged, snow-quieted water system.

Native brook trout hold out in the brook's wilder tributaries, and stocked ones feed in pools along its deeper, lower runs for at least a few weeks in spring. Edged by the white of yesterday's snow, open water and thinnest ice are jet black. Looked into from the right angle, these are windows to the trout's winter world. But in the brook's expanse of white ice and drifted snow, windows are few and far between; and within the interlacing miles of shielded January water, trout may be even fewer and farther between. In the deepest hold of the cold season, they have taken to overwintering niches. Trout, as well as many other stream and river fishes, seek shelter in slower currents with plentiful hiding places. In winter, trout take to concealment even more than they do in summer, and abundant cover is a primary habitat requirement. Another is water deep enough to keep them from the killing touch of ice yet with a low enough velocity that it does not exhaust them as they hold their stations until the thaw. Young-of-the-year brook trout are especially cryptic in winter, and may tunnel out of sight completely in thick mats of such aquatic plants as watercress. In the northern reaches of their range, brook trout parr (those in their first or second year of life) may hide themselves within the gravel or cobble substrate of the stream, an overwintering behavior they share with Atlantic salmon parr. As winter approaches, and water temperatures drop to the 40°–50°F range, some trout, particularly larger ones, move to deeper pools, a migration that is usually downstream, and can take them into rivers.

As I make my own migration downstream, the fragile covering of this run of water is not to be trusted, so I move among the alders, where the brook's floodplain has frozen solid. After several minutes of shuffling and rustling through the reed-grass, I come to the deep pool where this outlet brook joins the main stream. The liveliness of the water running down from the meadow keeps a small opening at its bubbling entrance to the pool, over which shelves, arches, and bridges of ice have been building throughout winter. Trout might well find this an agreeable overwintering niche. I try to look in, but snow-covered ice formations, broken water, and mazes of branches keep my eyes from penetrating the secretive depths of the pool. Its deep, slow side pockets are laced with silky dogwood branches that have been pulled into the water and held in place by the ice. Vines, grasses, leaves, and twigs snared from the current are woven by water into a subdued tapestry suspended from a loom of ice. Until spring's first thaw, fish

may hover within or beneath these shielding tangles, at times resting among the bottom stones.

I come upon beaver tracks in the snow, some distance from the brook, as I circle denser thickets on my way downstream. These animals have been at work in a stand of full-grown aspen. The area is trampled and patterned with their web-footed tracks, and scatterings of their wood chips are so recent that they have not begun to melt their way into the snow. I take the beaver trail thirty yards or so back to the brook, and see that it enters at the middle of a long stretch of riffles, where shallow water rushing and splashing over stones and gravel has prevented ice from forming. Trout, even young ones, will have nothing to do with this riffle-run in winter. Nor will they come to its churning dissolution in the head of the pool below it, or the midstream current it cuts through rock-lined pools on down the stream. These niches, likely feeding stations in warmer times, are abandoned in winter for the slower water along streambanks, the low-velocity reaches of runs, and deep still-water pools. In such retreats within the winter stream, holding positions about six inches above the substrate, trout will abide until spring. If conditions remain stable throughout the season of ice and snow, trout often wait in one place from December into late March.

Frost, ice, and snow. These and leaping water have been at work fashioning ice-sculptures along a swift, black-water run of the brook. The current keeps a narrow, serpentine channel open in the snow-silenced landscape of its descent. Somewhere in the leaden day the ice finds a jewel-like green with which to light its miniature palisades. Rocks that reach out of the dashing stream wear necklaces of ice and crowns of snow. Then all is level and drifted with snow where the icy work of winter has closed the surface of the deep, slow flow through alder and willow lowlands. There are no windows here. A fine snow begins to sift among the trees, with a crystal whisper in the slender twigs at my ear. Snow is being added to snow; my footprints begin to fill in behind me as I walk out from the brook.

The First of March: Hatching

Clear currents well and swirl at ice-openings; encircled by snow, fawn-colored islands of bare earth appear on southwest-facing slopes of the streambank. I walk from open space to open space along the banks and look into or fish the intermittent breaks in the ice cover of the brook. With cold February just ended, I want the sun of this first day of March full on my face, and so I abandon my custom of having the sun look over my shoulder, and work the water's eastern margins as the afternoon wears on. No sign of trout, not even a tug of line in the deeper pools. The winter quiet is broken only by the occasional sound of a ledge of snow dropping into the clear water. I can see deeply into the heart of this flow, all the way to the dark

bottom stones and gold-flecked gravel. The water seems alive, and appears to hold no life but its own. Yet there dwells in the brook, along its banks, within its bed, an abundance of life too hidden or too minute to be detected by a walker of its shores. Among this secret life are the tiny trout, the emerging fry who will be next autumn's bright, darting fingerlings. One could think that the stream creates full-size trout out of nothing more than sand, gravel, sunlight, and upwelling water. But the thousands of tiny, pearl-like eggs buried out of sight in gravel spaces and left to incubate in ever-flowing ice-water over the coldest season give rise to each year's class of brook trout. I have seen courtship displays among crimson-flanked males and radiant females arcing on their bronzed sides and fanning their tails over the gravel to clear out nesting redds. With the exception of the spring-spawning strains of rainbow trout, most salmonids breed in late autumn, as the chill deepens in the water and the hours of daylight diminish. Soon after the quivering pairs of speckled natives of this brook released their mingling milt and ova, their eggs settled into spaces in the gravel, became fertilized, and started developing into the tiny brook trout that began to emerge from their stony shelters late in February. The rate of development from fertilized egg to emergent fry depends on water temperatures and varies from species to species, and from one location to another. The process can take eight to nine months for autumn-spawning trout and char.

Because spawning in any given stream or river can occur over a period of weeks, and even as long as two months, and because temperatures can vary within a spawning area, the emergence of fry can be spread over considerable time. Even from a single egg pocket within a redd, the final baby fish to leave the gravel may be a couple of weeks behind the first. At the time they are deposited, trout eggs are slightly adhesive, which helps keep them from being dislodged from the pocket, which for most species is about a foot deep. These eggs soon swell and become turgid, losing their adhesiveness as they become wedged in place. An initial period of comparatively warmer water before the onset of winter temperatures is critical for a healthy start for the development of the embryonic fish. In the case of brook trout, the 40° to 55°F waters of late fall in which they spawn are sufficient for this initiation. A winter-long upwelling of water through interstices in the gravel is essential for providing oxygen to the embryos, and for preventing a suffocating buildup of sediments in the egg pocket. Water levels in spawning areas must remain fairly constant throughout incubation. Floods and ice scours can displace an entire streambed or dislodge the redds, annihilating an entire year's class of trout. This is particularly severe in the case of brook trout, a comparatively short-lived species that relies on a steady annual recruitment to maintain their populations. The formation of anchor ice, which builds up on bottom stones when the water temperature drops below freezing, is also fatal to nests. The best spawning sites for salmonids are in stable stretches of streams and rivers, where conditions stay nearly constant from the deposition of the eggs to the emergence of the fry. These parameters of the incubation period underscore the dependence these fish have on extensive favorable habitat.

Technically, hatching takes place at about the midpoint of the incubation process, in the heart of winter, when the embryonic trout breaks free of the egg's enclosing chorion and becomes a larval fish called an alevin. These young keep to their spaces down in the aggregate of tiny stones as they continue their development, nourished by a large yolk sac that provides fats, proteins, and carbohydrates. This attached food supply curtails movement, but the alevins will not be going anywhere for two months or so, at which time they will begin to emerge from the gravel as fry, fully formed replicas of their parent fish, a little under an inch and a quarter in length. As diminutive as they are at this point, they are trout, and ready to feed. And it seems that there is always something smaller in the water, something enough sizes down to serve the food chain's basic nourishing function. Their yolk sacs spent, trout fry begin

Brook trout alevin

foraging on algae, zooplankton, and similar minute organisms. Growth is fairly rapid, as they capture water fleas and diatomaceous life, graduating to underwater nymphs, larvae, and crustaceans. I have seen perfect crayfish in sizes down to invisibility in sidewaters along this brook.

In contrast with the high mortality accompanying the subsequent life stages of trout and char, the survival rate at this time of emergence is quite high, generally in the range of 80 to 90 percent. Forbidding survival rates more typical of salmonids come into play almost the moment the fry take leave of their redds, and only one or two out of a hundred will live to become the three- to four-inch fingerlings of September. Those who are first out of the redd have an advantage, as they have a head start in the critical area of growth, and are better able to defend the small territories they establish. Later in life, dominant trout defend favored feeding stations, and hierarchies are established among the trout in a stream; but in this emergent fry stage territoriality in its strictest sense is practiced, and the little trout strive to keep all others out of their space, their areas of use, at all times. Initial territories may be marked off in the gravel of the natal redd of the fry. In time they make their way along the stone, gravel, and sand substrate, in the lower current velocity of the stream bottom, to stone shelters in relatively shallow riffles or the quieter regions of side pockets away from the main flow.

Baby salmonids have two primary concerns: avoiding larger, predatory fish, and securing sufficient food to fuel the rapid growth requisite for survival. Many of the vulnerable fry are lost to predation, but starvation may be an even greater mortality factor as the restrictive realities of salmonid life in a stream are brought to bear. There is only so much suitable habitat available, only so much food, and competition for these finite resources is severe. In a very real sense, space equals food to these dwellers of ever-drifting waters. On the threshold of the fullness of spring, a great thinning-out of the youngest takes place with trout, as it does with so many animals. Size, a significant factor in all stages of a trout's life, is paramount during the first weeks. Smaller, often weaker fry are driven from desirable niches by dominant members of their own hatchling class, who themselves may be little more than an inch long. The smallest can be forced to struggle in the swifter, more difficult flows where capturing prey is too challenging, and where exhaustion settles in. They are left with no place to hide, and are more vulnerable to predation. Denial of access to the stream's food resources may take the heaviest toll. Energy demands are high, and the tiny trout are unable to endure the periods of fasting an older, larger trout could survive. They are quick to weaken, becoming even less able to take prey or avoid predation. The command to grow is so imperative that even dominant fry frequently forsake protected places, risking their nascent lives in a constant quest for food. The instinct to keep to cover, so compelling throughout subsequent years of a brook trout's life, is subordinated during these first weeks or months to the demand for growth, until a threshold size is achieved, at which they retreat to hidden places they will be thereafter reluctant to forsake. Later in their first year, those young trout who survive this settling-out, in an intriguing reversal of territorial behavior, will tend to join others of the same year-class and keep to schools in the shallow sidewaters off to the edge of the channel's main flow.

At this point, any backwaters still lie under shields of ice. Only the most turbulent sections of the swiftest races are open water. It is all but impossible to imagine the newborn of any animal, however suited to its environment, coming to life 'in ground-up stone and ice-water in this winter brook's first inclination toward spring. A trout's nest certainly cannot be thought of in terms of the often-humanized bird's nest. These stippled, silver shivers of life are on their own, holding places out of currents rushing with the thrust of the thaw. They are far too small to keep a place in the swift and steady surge of a brook at its full, racing to join a river.

The fry must stay behind stones, move through bottom gravel, make their way to quieter swirls and drifts on watery shelves along the brook-edge. Here, in the manner of trophy trout of deeper, wilder waters, they will take up feeding stations immediately downcurrent of their own equivalents of boulders, logs, and undercut banks; or in riffles and runs of low-gradient meanders where water plants such as watercress and fountain moss, green throughout the winter, protect them from predators and the stream's relentless sweep. Obstructions and slower currents along the margins of streams and rivers are essential for the survival of fry; the more complex and varied these lateral habitats are, the more favorable the habitat is for the continuance of trout. Though roofed over by sheaths of ice, such places abound along this brook. It will be a while before I catch my first sight of this year's new brook trout along their awakening waterway. I can be patient with the knowledge that they are here, and leave the March sun to begin its season-changing work on ice and snow.

Opening World: The Thaw

A pine-tree wind dusts his sleeves and coat; • a pebbly stream cleans his heart and ears.

—Li Po

Thaw: 5 March

The day goes down in stillness and sharp cold on rose-colored snow. An ocher late-afternoon light briefly warms the landscape before it pales to winter white and then to a quickly darkening sky. With the sun's descent the snow stiffens, and the sound of my footsteps changes. Trees go black along the brook; winter stars will decorate the sky. However chill it has been, daylight has lingered surprisingly, and its gain of three minutes for the day does not seem a true accounting of the advance. There will be another two minutes added tomorrow at sunrise, a minute or two at sunset. These measurings of the season have been in effect for some days now, though lengthening days tend to go unnoticed until a startling accumulation is achieved. But the brook has taken note of these fractions since the longest night of the year. No time seems to pass, nothing seems to happen, but there are constant progressions and the brook today is not the same brook it was yesterday. Differences register in the knowing possessed by all things within the brook and along the brook. The water itself seems to have a knowledge. Spillways at the beaver dam have a louder voice than at my last passing, and trickling silver laces the lowland alder stands where I marveled at crystalline ledges only days ago.

The season is astir. I am perplexed by

the at once cyclical and ever-advancing nature of this and all seasons, the way they seem to circle and return, and yet each that has passed has moved somewhere out in time, as though analogous with the manner in which the planets circle the sun and galaxies wheel, while ever moving outward in space and time. For this moment I depart a winter wood and its snow-bound brook, knowing I ride a wheel toward spring.

6 March: Blackwater Brook

Silence near noon, stillness and silence. A few chickadees call now and again, and when they sing it is their heart-gladdening spring song. They attend the alders that line this straight run of Blackwater Brook, an open reach on level land that eventually makes a sharp and sudden turn and meanders west, with deep pools and undercut banks for two miles or so, before straightening out through a wooded stretch until it finds its way into the south-flowing river. The landscape is snowbound still as I walk an old railroad bed to a rise where the brook narrows and its acres of backwaters are funneled into a natural channel. The water rushes with wild agitation before quieting again to slide along its course and, at this time of high water, flood and drift through the bordering wetlands. The narrow surge is where the ice opens first, and is one of my central sites for looking into the heart of the brook each spring.

It is a cold but lively heart. Its swirls race and pulse, and work against the ice. The water seems one and many and, having freed itself to make this little run in open air, appears impatient with the bonds of winter. Sluicing, eddying, leaping over itself at times, cutting back against its own insistent flow, in league with the strengthening sun and warming sweeps of wind, the brook erodes the ice that bounds it. Upstream as well as downstream, as far as I can see, there is snow cover.

The opening-up will have to come soon. The low light of winter's shortened days has been diminished even further as it has had to find its way through thickening accretions of snow and ice. Each pelting of sleet and sifting of snow, each advancing of the ice into the depths has dimmed the light in the water. Life processes in the stream, from the microscopic up, already greatly suppressed by near-freezing water temperatures, are reduced all the more in the absence of light. For trout and other aquatic animals who feed (however infrequently) in winter, there can be a shortage of prey. In ice-covered, still-water regions, oxygen can become depleted when plants are unable to utilize photosynthesis. The water's energetic mingling with the air at this ice-opening serves a valuable aerating function.

I look into the shallowest section along the narrows, into a dizzying play of gold and amber lights in swirling dark water, where I can make out the wavering shape of several stones. Trout would not be inclined to pass here at this season. If they were to, I'd not be likely to make them out,

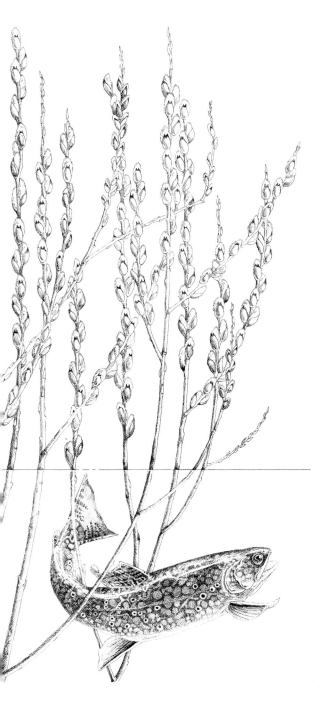

though the remotest possibility and the hypnotic lightshow in the water at thaw keep me staring into this one opening into the realm of the trout. Trout that I see near the surface here in late spring and early summer could be wintering deep below, holding to the slower water of the bottom and the banks. The brook is 38°F; wherever they have retreated for the winter the trout continue to hold and wait, hovering brightly, tails sweeping and fins flicking from time to time, all but immobile, but inwardly alert to every rising degree.

I lie on an old bridge that crosses the stream and look into the water; my bare hands appreciate the warmth in the wooden structure, and the back of my neck feels the agreeable burn of the late winter sun, which in a matter of days will become the early spring sun. I am broken away from the swirling water's hypnotic hold and brought to my feet by a distant bird call. I am certain I have heard a red-winged blackbird. Yet one call only, and apparently from a solitary bird, does not seem to suit the flocking habit of this species. An advance male perhaps, in the cattail or sweetgale stands—but there is no other call. I could think I dreamed it. I cross the bridge, descend into alder thickets along the channel's flood margin, and thread my way to the edge of the frozen water, my eyes searching for an opening in the snow cover, my ears alert for a red-winged blackbird song that never comes. Where ice abuts the rising bank, I find a window of black ice. I kneel for a look into shallow water, where everything is remarkably clear and still. A larva undulates by, in the narrow water layer between the ice and the leaf-strewn bottom. Another swims into my view, several more, and then a steady stream of them. These are mayfly larvae. There is life, rather vibrant life, in water only several degrees away from becoming frozen solid. Clouds of swimming larvae fill my ice window, presaging their future swarming dances as mayflies in milder air, at the times of the hatches. I cannot imagine what means of energy can propel these wriggling bits of life, or the dark, round beetle that streaks by, through this winter water. And deep in water equally cold, trout at times break from their winter holding patterns with sudden, swift moves to take the crawling, darting nymphs that are their sustenance over the cold season. I ease myself carefully onto thicker ice at the deepwater's edge. I have not the least desire to drop into the world of the trout at this point of the year. Here the brook is closed over by a gray, glacial shelf, a layering of frozen brook water, sleet, snow, and hail. Wherever the current has sheared a section of this shelving, its striations reveal a compressed history of the winter's storms above the brook. On the arctic crust at my feet I see a number of leaves, twigs, and tiny seeds that have taken heat from the winter sun and gradually burned their way three to four inches deep into the ice shelf, straight down, etching a perfect cutout of themselves into the lead-gray matrix. The far sun and the near earth, their living and nonliving components, are in a more direct dialogue, literally a more intimate touch with one another, than anything we commonly imagine.

Ice Scour: 17 March

After a walk along a high, wooded bank I look in on the river from a narrow two-lane bridge. Cloud-shreds streak the sky, and the calls of restless crows break down from higher ridges. Snow holds on all but the south-facing slopes. The chill first day of spring draws near; the equinox is at that strange turning of some dark corner far out in space that works with time and light, and will return, in barely perceptible installments, day's advantage over night. The river comes to life, sections of it roar. After a winter of strange groanings in the night, imitations of whale songs and gunshots, the great bed of restless ice breaks free. Huge chunks of ice, loosened by fingers of sunlight that would seem too feeble yet to effect such great work, spin slowly as they ride the water-rush I look down upon. The bridge shudders with the crushing impacts of these ice-cakes. Impeded for a moment, they ride up over one another, grinding and crushing, breaking away blinding white edges that go gray in the black water's embrace. The gradual inclination back toward the sun by the northern latitudes releases winter's store of snow and ice, some as harmless trickles, some as violent scours and floods that threaten the lives of the stream dwellers. The passing winter has been one to favor ice buildup, and spring breakup will make the river, and all its tributaries, all but unfishable. Ice scour is perhaps the greatest peril faced by trout of rivers and streams. As floods of frigid water bearing crowbars and mauls of ice surge downstream at thaw, they can shift boulders and rearrange the very streambed. Entire year-classes of eggs and alevins can be lost as the scouring flood churns its way though the spawning gravel. Older trout who have taken refuge in flood plains and their tributaries can be crushed or suffocated by the collapse of thick spans of accumulated ice and snow, or become stranded when temporary sanctuaries of backwaters entrapped by ice dams are suddenly drained as these dams are torn away. A waterway's entire food chain can be ripped away by the forceful surge of the thaw, and take seasons to recover.

Spring Equinox: 20 March

Primavera, the first sweet day of spring. The sleet that slants against me seems appropriate to spring equinox—precipitation halfway between snow and rain, marking the day that divides daylight and darkness equally. The season, which begins officially at ten P.M. tonight, will have to work awhile. But the ice is off the brook, and the water is wildly alive. I see no fish in the deeper pools in which I suspect that some, including trout, abide the winter. Broken water and gray March sky-glare make the brook all but impossible to read. The water temperature is 38°F here.

Warming Brook: 29 March

I have returned to rushing Deer Brook after a day and night of heavy rain. Lingering snowbanks have been washed from the hollows on the north side of stones. Snow that was blue-shadowed silence all winter long now sings as one of the brook's thousand silver tongues. The air temperature is 50°F, even on a misty day; it is moss-weather, and on boulders and tree roots the mosses have an emerald glow. The brook is no longer fed by the melting of ice and snow, but by rain and mist formed in warming air. The brook is now 44°F. I would not know this without a thermometer. My hand went painfully numb in today's water just as quickly as it did a week ago. But the trout are no doubt keenly aware of this increment of 6°, and must have their ways of rejoicing in it.

Opening Day: 1 April

This year, opening day brings back something of the earlier, more aboriginal fisherman in me. The significance of this specific date has become lost as other scales of time and the seasons have become my icons: the first black amoebas of open water in the white streamscape, the first tricklings of water loosened by the thaw to seek their way down rocky slopes, the first clear look at bottom gravel in sun-slants penetrating clear runs of meltwater. There are no living things at this point, only the streams themselves literally springing to life. I have walked the brooks where the water has kept its heartbeat, as the trout within it have kept their heartbeats, through the cold season. Today I go to the lake, the great lake where winter lingers on above and beneath a forbidding mantle of ice. This world of water has been closed to the world of air for months. Now, as the glacial veil is driven back by the wind and the steepening angle of the sun, small fish move in silvery clouds toward the first open daylight of the surface waters, and bigger fish rise from the depths to chase them. A hook through the fragile tail of a rainbow smelt cast into the narrow fishable margin between miles of land and miles of ice might catch in the jaw of a metallic, black-flecked Atlantic salmon, a landlocked one who will never see his namesake ocean. Either of two other prizes might be drawn forth from the awakening lake: a rose-and-lavender rainbow trout, or a light-spotted, green-gray lake trout.

Yet despite the lure of an opening-day catch, I cannot seem to make this great lake an extension of my habitat, though I make sporadic attempts to do so. I am out of my element here, in part because of nat-

ural aspects of the lake: its oceanic vastness, which to some is an inspiring challenge, but translates to foreboding inaccessibility for me; the unforgiving climate of all but the best and briefest times here; and the brooding, frigid depths, in which no plant familiar to me can grow. These are all things that, in the ocean itself, turn me back to shallower inland waters after an initial period of strange and mysterious pull, a surreal enchantment. My feelings of being an alien here have roots in unnatural factors as well: as enormous as it is, the lake is virtually surrounded by human constructs. However artfully left standing or introduced, well-pruned specimen trees and exotic shrubs appear awkward in the landscape, and cannot conceal rooflines, glassy-eyed expanses of window forever watching the water, open lawns, and spreads of pure white sand. This endless vision eats at my heart and spirit more bitingly than the snow-bearing wind off the ice-covered lake eats at the warmth I try to keep within me. And this is before the boats are loosed on the water.

But the falling snow does a magical

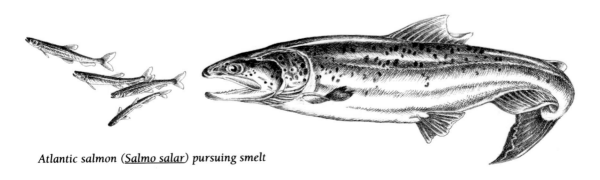

Atlantic salmon (<u>Salmo salar</u>) pursuing smelt

thing, obscuring the shorelines while leaving visible the crests of distant hills and the tops of a few towering, wind-wracked pines. I am here on opening day because of a remembered fascination, a personal history I do not feel is all that ancient but that predates many rooflines, and the invitation of my son, who has not become so hounded by the houses around the lake that he cannot stand to come here. He can overlook the encircling habitations and see only the great sheet of glacial ice with its receding rim being opened up by wind and waves, and imagine the fish below. Nor does he need a blinding squall to make himself feel alone, or to see the lake and its elusive, mysterious fish as truly wild.

We fish first from a crowd of rocks in a section of shallows on private land, to which my son has been granted access. The natural opening here is several square feet, through which two live-baited hooks are introduced, with the hope that they will be taken within range of the splendid salmonids who stir somewhere out there. This site provides a welcome measure of solitude, ensured by the snow. But no message of fish is sent back along thin lines reeled off beneath the ice. One large shape phantoms by in the dark, snow-eating water, and hearts race nearly enough to warm fingertips, but a long while of silence and cold, snow and windsweep, follow. We move on. As I struggle with stiff fingers to make my gear transportable, I think of those who fish interminably with ice on their reels, and admire their endurance and their devotion to the link they have with the ice-animals they seek in water a degree or two away from becoming solid. Searching for any means by which I can upgrade my metabolism, I volunteer to carry the heavy bucket of ice-water in which the lively, radiant baitfish swim.

We have no trouble finding room at the little town dock. There is something to be said for a harsh climate. Like the refugee ospreys and eagles who come here so rarely now that each appearance is a news-making occasion, we have come here to try for a fish in the comparative quiet of one of the most impossible times. Forty or fifty yards of open water from shore to the edge of the ice, by a two-hundred-yard-or-so stretch of shoreline; this fishable extent represents perhaps one-millionth of the lake's area. Three rods lean against the guardrail at the end of the dock, watched from shore by three down-jacketed figures in the cabs of three trucks with their motors running. A solitary figure, dressed as a rummage sale, huddles against the railing, immobile, holding a rod under a thick-sleeved arm. There is no hand in sight. Presuming him to be alive, we do not intrude upon his space.

The fact that they are catching nothing and indicate that they have caught nothing does not seem to hold significance for us as we bait up and send smelt on a limited swim in a limitless lake. I think back and try to remember the "being there" feeling that sent me out on opening days earlier in my life, when mist and rain every bit as cold as snow marked the longed-for April day, and try to recapture some of that spirit. But the quickening wind runs out of squalls, the swirling white fades away, and my heart drops as rooftops reappear and the cove becomes small and sad in the early spring sun. One can become discouraged with life and lack of fish, and fish on; but one cannot fish with half a heart. And yet, for all my profound misgivings, there is a lure here for me. It is the fish, and simply thoughts of them. I would not be here to watch the ice melt. What if a streaking salmon were to take my line, or a rainbow trout shattered the wind-riffled surface, trying to dislodge my hook? What if Namaycush, "dweller of the deep," as the Native Americans called the lake trout, began to pull me toward the depths? What if one last char, one of the race that had held out in the deepest recesses of this lake since the departure of the glaciers 11,000 years ago but that has been extirpated in recent times by the activities of the European settlers, somehow remained here, and took my hook so that I could coax him briefly to the surface, look him in the eye, and admire the red speckling and sharp white fin-edges so reminiscent of his brother brook trout? I keep my eyes and thoughts to the near-at-hand and dream of fish. There is only the awakening lake lapping at the shore, the receding rim of ice, the twitch-awaiting tip of my rod, with its hairlike line trailing away to invisibility in the realm of the trout.

April Rain: 5 April

Pussy willows are in full bloom in the hollows. Their silver-white flowers hold yellow pollen, and they shed black bud scales down on me as I brush through them. These heavily catkinned shrubs show a trust in the season's advance, as do the peepfrogs, with their shrill pipings. The welcome, season-heralding calls of these tiny frogs punctuate the murmur of light rain in the willow-alder thickets. Some distance from the brook, I hear the rush of water. Every stream is swollen, and even hillside rivulets two inches deep run and splash as if they will flow forever. Thaw and spring rains, then the great rush of water and the living tide that comes with it: a bird or two, amorous newts in marshy backwaters, a solitary peeper, then the chorus and movement of all these

Rainbow smelt (<u>*Osmerus mordax*</u>*)*

living things in numbers impossible to count. Above the roar of the brook I hear the raucous sound of a wood-frog orgy. They will fill their vernal pools with eggs in a matter of a few days, then leave the water and take up life in the moist, fern-shaded woods along the brooks. The beauty and grace of quicksilver trout are woven more boldly now in flowing streams in which a thousand things enliven. A day and night of rain have passed, April rain; another 6° for the brook, and now the water is 50°F. Trout are on the move.

Tannery Brook: 7 April

Today I walk up into the foothills, north to Tannery Brook, where I can follow the rushing spring-melt as it leaps among mossy rock and twisting tree roots on its way to the level land below. A March-like wind sets the upper trees to swirling in a sort of circle-dance, with swaying torsos and sweeping arms; below, where I walk, their trunks are staid, their feet firmly planted. And here the water does its own dance. So recently a vein of ice in a winter forest, the brook is set to running among rocks and roots. April sun-slants touch them all, and at a moment like this it is hard to say what is living and what is nonliving, among trees and stones, moss and water, the wind and me. To these could be added the sun and the trout I seek.

I first came here years ago, led by a younger friend who was just about done being a boy. Way has led on to way and I don't know where the man lives now. Perhaps he comes back, as I do, on rare occasions. I have kept the secret he shared with me, and have never seen a sign of anyone's being here. It is usually easy to know whether or not a stream is fished. When I do return I remember him, his movements, mostly. He slipped among the buttressed trees and tangled thickets, over and around rocks, like a mink along the banks and over the brook. He didn't step, leap, or skip, exactly, he scurried in a springy crouch over the slippery terrain, surefooted and nearly invisible. He maneuvered his fishing rod as though he were fencing; it never got in his way. I suppose he was a trout's bad dream, a mink with a hook and line. But although that was nearly a quarter of a century ago, and the loss of native trout and their habitat, and angling pressure were not yet severe problems in this region, he spaced his fishing well, in time and distance, and never was a real threat to the secretive native trout of this diminutive brook. My own movements were, as they are now, slow and fairly long on stealth, if short on grace. Oddly enough, several years later, when the time came for me to teach my son something of how to fish such brooks for trout, he quickly developed the minklike manner of my friend, who he never knew. Their style of furtive swiftness allowed these two to cover the streamside more rapidly than I. And as neither of them was as inclined to lean among the trees out over the water for long periods of time, they were more efficient at taking trout. It might never have occurred to me to fish this little brook. For much of its length, it is no "brook too broad for leaping." I can step across it in many places. And had I fished it without my young guide, I might never have caught a trout, running a line through the lively riffles or intermittent pools. The fish here keep to the trees, and my friend knew that.

I edge up to the brook. Its racing water rushes so loudly I cannot hear my booted feet in last autumn's leaves. Perhaps I have come too early. The brook is close to 50°F. A colder reading would not have surprised me, for this wildly falling water is still mingled with runoff snow-melt from the slopes, and I recall everything being cold here well into June. Tannery Brook seems to collect water from everywhere in the time of thaw as it seeps in from the banks, flows over gravel washouts, bubbles up from springs, and splashes in from tiny tributaries that will have dried up by the end of May. Here I feel closer to the origin of the brook, closer to the ice-water sources of its cold-water trout. I would sense this even more so if I were to ascend higher into these hills,

and the mountains that crown them. In such places the common and scientific names of the native trout are most apt. They are indeed "brook" trout, at one with that element. They are also both "Salvelinus," an old name for arctic-loving char and indicative of "little salmon," and "fontinalis," which signifies "living in cold springs."

As I descend from pool to occasional pool I wonder if the trout have reclaimed them after the roaring waters and ice scour of the initial thaw subsided, or if they were able to find shelter in them throughout the long winter. In brooks like this, their comings and goings are all the more mysterious, as they appear, disappear, and reappear with the stresses and vicissitudes of the seasons, from ice scour and flood to heat and drought. Even in more stable stream environs, wild trout populations can undergo

*Wood frog (*Rana sylvatica*)*

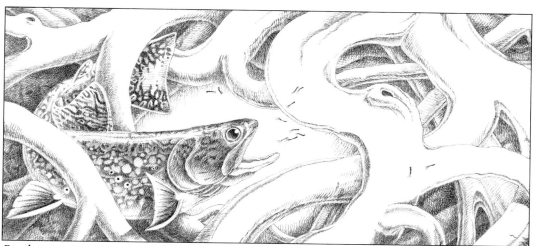
Brook trout among tree roots

extreme variations as a result of natural conditions. The small natives of a brook like this live on the edge a good deal of the time, their survival dependent upon the narrowest of margins. Short-lived by nature, they would seem to press their luck in such volatile habitats. Ice scour must be devastating here, some years. As many as seven generations of these "little char of the cold springs" have lived and died since the first time I came to Tannery Brook.

When I come to more level ground, I fish among the trees, recalling the first trout I saw taken here, a glimmering eight- or nine-inch speckled fish my friend pulled, as if by magic, from a black hole among the holdfasts of red maple and yellow birch. No casting or retrieving here, certainly. All was cautious approach and careful dropping of the baited hook or weighted nymph, and letting it ride and dance on upwelling or eddying water, or deftly jigging in dead

pockets, presentations in their own right. He seemed to know just where, and how, to hook a trout, catching a fish without losing a leader, and it seemed he tried only where there was indeed a trout. I worked no such magic. The trees and tangles I tried all seemed devoid of fish, and I spent a lot of time replacing hooks. It could be that my step was too heavy, or that I was not careful enough with my shadow. Trout were there, and obviously hungry, though it may have been earlier in the season than my quest today. Then, as happens with matters such as fishing—of desire necessitating skill, or at least finding a way—the time, the touch, and the place all seemed right. Fishing blind from behind a red maple, I felt that tug for which I had waited all winter, that first unmistakable pull that was no trick of current, stone, or sunken branch, nor of my own imagination. And so I came to fish among tree roots, the reaching, writhing forms that look like water held in place, their cell-by-cell advance and thickening over time tracing a course nearly as penetrating and winding as that of water. Among these snakelike branchings, hidden in holes and pockets, trout hold themselves in place and wait for drifting prey.

I move through the shadows of budding trees and step as lightly as I can, though I feel the rush and tumble of this brook at thaw will mask my presence. Still, it is best never to underestimate the extraordinary senses of trout, the awareness they possess. To spend one hour within and so intently attuned to a brook in spring would be mind-altering. I try, as best I can, through the trout that are their living embodiments and the magic of the water itself, to know these streams a little. Shivering with the wind and the excitement that always comes with the season's or the day's first committing a line to water, I extend the tip of my rod just beyond the edge of the brook and drop into a swirl in the midst of a tangle of roots. A take, or was it a snag, merely? Thinking back to former days here, I dip into several eddies, braids, and still waters, anywhere the brook cuts back in under its banks or the buttresses of the trees. And then comes a well-remembered pulling of the line. I set the hook and draw the fish forth quickly; there is no playing a trout in these tangles. I catch a glimpse of the little native, maybe six inches long, as he thrashes just beneath the surface, a flash of a look at a flash of a trout. He slips away, this lightly hooked little one, gone without trace in the continuing splay and splash of water. These electrifying moments among hours of walking and wading, of working a line or merely watching, are spaced in time, spaced in the stream of the day itself, as the trout are spaced in the streaming waters that hold them. There is always disappointment when a trout is lost—we seek to find, after all, not to lose—but it is better that this little one is free so easily. I had wanted to see a trout, to catch one. I have caught and seen and lost one. There is a ritual in this. It is another spring. Spring is here and the brook is running wild and free; trout are here and I am here. These strong and valiant survivors of winter ice and summer drought, these alert, swift, and agile animals who can live on the edge of glaciers and find food in waterfalls, and who dodge the beaks of herons and the talons of eagles, are so cryptic within their environment, and so fragile out of it, that they can rarely be seen alive. And if a trout is taken, and killed, its colors and even its form fade so quickly that the beholding is momentary only, the vision as ephemeral as the final splendid minutes of a sunset. One can gather the most delicate of the spring wildflowers, but cannot collect these brilliant bits of living water. Even with hands wet to numbness in the waters of the thaw, to hold trout is to burn them.

I have come to this little brook to see if it is the same as I remember. It is for one more season at least. I come to these unspoiled brooks, which are like promises kept, to be among them and celebrate their seasons. On this occasion I also come to fish. I reach across the brook with my rod and dip along a shelf of yellow-birch roots, then let a run of line take off with the sparkling current. The line straightens with a brook trout's seizing. I set the hook, and draw a dogged fish through the rippling water. A good one for the keeping, and it seems this brook can yet bear some fishing, so I walk on and fish, seeking the three more that will provide a dinner. The rocking of the trees has died away in the settling down of the wind, and afternoon inclines toward twilight as I catch the last supper-trout.

As I turn away from the damp, mossy borders of the brook, where skunk cabbage has thrust forth flower-shielding hoods, and shuffle through the wind-dried leaves on the forest floor, I think of the irony in the name Tannery Brook. Tanneries were a major factor in the decline of the native brook trout and the sharp reduction of its range, as forests were stripped of hemlocks to provide the acid for tanning the hides of buffalo being exterminated and cattle being propagated by the thousands in the 1800s. Coupled with the wholesale clear-cutting of northeastern forests throughout the same era, this effectively degraded the ecology of the region's streams and rivers forever. With the loss of the critical shading provided by the crowns of hemlock and white pine, and the capacity for retention of cold spring water in the

root systems of these trees, all the waterways inhabited by trout ran warmer. This habitat degradation was exacerbated by accompanying erosion and siltation, and the scouring of rivers by miles of sawn logs. Salmonids that had survived the scourings of glaciers over millennia were destroyed within decades by crushing rivers of timber, the eradication of riparian habitat, and the building of dams. The original range of the brook trout, which reached from the mouth of Hudson Bay to headwater streams as far south as Georgia and South Carolina, and west to northern Iowa, was drastically constricted, and has been dwindling ever since. Within remaining native habitat, they have withdrawn to the far north, or the remotest

Skunk cabbage (Symplocarpus foetidus)

33

holdouts, as their world has been taken away and they have been subjected to fishing pressure that their survival and reproductive rates cannot withstand.

Far below, along Tannery Brook's deeper run, a sawmill crumbles in the midst of dense, sprouting hemlocks. My friend caught several natives in the twelve-inch class there, in pools under old planking and stonework. The mill died out. The tannery is gone. The largest trout are gone. But far upstream the woods have come back, and native brook trout, however reduced in circumstance, persist. I may not come back here myself. At least not to fish. This is one of those last places, those places on the edge now. So much has changed in the twenty-three years that have passed since a young friend showed me how to fish tree roots.

Riffles: 9 April

Pressing my way through thicketed slopes, I approach a section of Deer Brook where the crescendo of a waterfall at full spring flood has now dropped away to a trio of silver tongues of mid-April runoff. The seasons have their separate voices in the stream. April splashes pure water now, without the tones of ice and snow. The whispering of a quieter reach's slides and swirls against the banks becomes lost in the murmur of the spillway I steal upon. Here, where water levels rise and fall abruptly over the course of the year, is where the brook works out its tone poems in endless theme and variation.

I am detained by the riffles; their play of light and sound is a joyful prelude to the warm season. The energetic upheaval and broken water here would be enough to conceal any young trout holding in a hollow among the stones and gravel beneath the animated surface. This tumbling of the water provides more than brook-sounds: it is a critical source of food and cover for stream-dwelling trout. Ranging in depth from an inch to three feet or so, riffles are sections of brooks and rivers where turbulence created by water flowing over gravel, cobbles, or boulders on the streambed reaches to the surface. In this agitation of the current, air and water mix, and gases are absorbed and swept beneath the surface. For salmonids, one of the most important benefits of this lively dialogue between water and air is the oxygen brought into the stream, as well-aerated water is essential for all of their activities. This vital gas never approaches in water the concentration it holds in the atmosphere; even in air-saturated plunge-pools the concentration of oxygen is less than one percent. In addition to their role in aeration, riffles are food-producers in a stream. Even where forest canopies restrict sunlight from penetrating these shallow, turbulent runs, many aquatic insects find their niches. These invertebrates are components of a food chain based on a delayed bounty from the sun, the cascades of autumn leaves, and fallen streamside bark, twigs, ferns, sedges, and grasses. Wherever sunlight is able to reach into riffles, abundant food chains arise, from algae to minnows, which provide sustenance for trout and other larger stream animals. Insects are one part of this food chain, and they flourish beneath the surface of this roiling water. Some of these, such as certain species of mayflies, have extremely flattened bodies and can exist in the narrow margins between swift water and the smooth surface of a stone. Others, like blackfly larvae, manage to attach themselves in some of the strongest flows. These tiny creatures, soon to hatch into tenth-of-an-inch adults, in swarming clouds that will antagonize my late-spring wanderings, spin silken mats on rocks and then hook themselves into these unyielding mats by means of specialized prolegs. The blackfly larvae then extend themselves into the thin, slow-water boundary immediately above the rock and reach food-collecting fans into the swift stream. Trout feed on these minute larvae, though they may feed more often on larger aquatic prey such as caddis larvae, stonefly nymphs,

and minnows, who in their turn feed on the blackfly larvae. Sunlight piercing moving water to touch a stone, or a trapped leaf disintegrating in the stream can initiate a complex of life from phytoplankton to caddis flies and mayflies, two favored foods of trout and inspiration for countless designs and devices fashioned on hooks by those who fish for trout.

As the rush of thaw and April runoff quiets along these riffles, stretches of them will drop to depths of an inch to six inches, and they will become one of the younger trout's most valued refuges, for here they will be able to forage safely, under cover of broken water, and in flows too shallow to permit the entrance of predatory larger trout. Adults themselves can hold in riffles at depths over a foot, if lulls can be found in the current. A number of species of small minnows and suckers, as well as darters and sculpin, bottom-huggers all, who keep out of the current by lurking behind or beneath

Caddis larva (Pycnopsyche sp.)

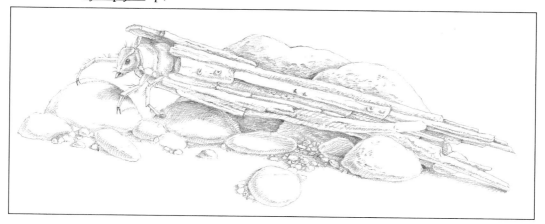

stones, also inhabit the animated waters of these productive microenvironments. Water finding its circuitous way over gravel, stones, or boulder-studded sand, in narrow brook channels or broad river reaches, establishes patterns of riffles and pools, the quintessential habitat of trout.

Yearling: 11 April

A yearling brook trout drifts speckled and golden in the amber water, over dark stones and light gravel. He is on a spring sally in a tranquil sidewater, at the head of Royal Fern Pool. His shadow, in the perfect form of a diminutive trout, follows beneath and just behind him.

I seldom see an unhurried trout. A young trout is so much an aspect of the sun-lit stream that he can vanish by simply holding still, his stippled pattern becoming lost among flickers of light and glimmers in gravel and sand, his black, smudgy marks merging with the dark places among the stones and slender branch-shadows in the brook. The dark, oblong blotches along his sides will decorate and camouflage him into his second year of life, a coloration he shares with Atlantic salmon and a number of other salmonid species. Fish marked like this in their juvenile stage are known as parr.

The young brook trout, nearly four inches long, keeps to the sunlight of the open water as he calmly glides by my crouching place along the shore, his apparent insouciance belying the forbidding mortality rate for baby trout and the rigors of winter in a stream that he had to surmount in order to sparkle in this clear water on this

Sculpin (Cottus sp.)

day. Out of every one thousand eggs committed to redds by brook trout spawning in any given autumn, about twenty of the young-of-the-year who emerge the following spring will survive until September. Of those twenty who enter their first winter as fingerlings, perhaps eight or ten will live through to spring and take up their second summer of growth. A half dozen of these may go on to become two- or three-year-olds. By this time, they are already growing old, and senescence becomes a limiting factor for these relatively short-lived fish. It is likely that only one or two will reach ages three or four. With the exception of uncommon strains in a few waters of northern latitudes, such as Assinica Lake and the Broadback River in Quebec, whose larger, later-maturing brook trout can live seven to ten years, members of this species rarely live to ages five or six.

The adventurer below me turns in sun-slants, ascends to circle stones, then rises and hovers at mid-depth, about six inches above the substrate of the brook. He does not appear to be foraging, for he has his back to the current's drift, though the water here is essentially unmoving. For a few moments he has apparently set aside his quest for food. He may have fed well enough in the riffles just upstream to be free for a moment from the compelling need to capture prey. This need will be a constant of his life, although as he fills out he will be better able to endure the periods of fasting dictated by less favorable times. This yearling has done well to have put a summer of growth behind him, and to have made it through his first winter. His poise and movements suggest a confident advance reflecting the season's own mood. The time of thaw, with its wild upheavals along the banks and in the restless brook, levels out, and a trout-favoring time settles in. April rains may yet bring spates and turbid floodwaters, but the yearling trout, not long since a fingerling, has a history with his stream, and will be equal to its seasonal challenges. This bright and fluid young brook trout is one of the eight or ten in a thousand left from last year's hatching. He is at a turning point, even as the season is at a turning point.

The yearling appears at home as he moves into twists of root and tangles of sunken branches. He is, in fact, at home, in all likelihood beginning to define a place for himself within the stream and among the other trout who hold their places in its floating, drifting world. The parr edges into shadow…one last appearance in a shaft of sunlight, and he is out of sight in the undercuts and submersed brush. He knows this pool already, this long, deep, shrub-shielded pool beneath the alders. I do not fish here. This seven-mile run of water is for the most part a succession of precipitous, narrow spillways out of the hills, tumbling down over moss-rocked cascades in deep woodland shade. Deer Brook harbors what appears to be a limited population of native trout, and most reaches can support only those in the six-inch class or so. From time to time I see sizable trout in the extensive lower run, its final flow before emptying into the river. But there cannot be many. I keep this a watching-stream.

Those parr who survive their high-risk first year will take up a foraging site downstream of the older trout who dominate this pool, or they may take position off to one side in a site such as the one into which this particular yearling has just disappeared. He will stay out of sight of the larger trout, but align himself to keep a watchful eye on the same drift corridor, waiting for an insect to be brought within his range. He will also be mindful of any stirring on the bottom of the brook. The yearling will test and reject many more of the specks carried within or on the surface of the current than a mature trout would; much of what is seized will not prove edible, and will be spit back

out. There is only so much time to discern a form advancing in or on the water, and to intercept the potential prey. The parr will learn, in time, to detect acceptable prey before taking it into his mouth, becoming capable of making split-second decisions in a split-second world. It is here that the essence of the contest between the salmonids and those who fish for them has its origins.

I wait; the yearling does not reappear. There are dimplings in the water against the bank, but I cannot tell if it is a fish at work, let alone what kind of fish it might be. There is nothing in the sunlit center of the pool. The white suckers have yet to make their migration here, moving up from

Brook trout parr

38

their wintering grounds in the river to begin their lazy turnings and nosings in the bottom debris. There is no sign of the schools of minnows and dace that so often sweep by here, a living current streaming against the water's flow.

Resplendent, yet camouflaged, in sunlight and shadow, the yearling has taken to overhead cover. He will keep to it, now that he has reached this modest size, for the remainder of his life in this stream. He will want lacings of leaves and twigs throughout the air above his foraging station, branch-tangles and trailing bankside vegetation at the surface, or an earth-shelf of the bank itself overhanging his holding lie; he will keep something always overhead, except for those darting instants of seizing prey. A year following their hatching, trout generally enter a season of rapid growth, and as their body length increases, the area of their feeding territory is expanded proportionally. If the year now responding to the promise of spring proves a favorable one for this hidden trout of Royal Fern Pool, he could reach a length of six or seven inches from his snout to the fork of his nearly square tail by the end of September. And by the time the leaves that have yet to break out of their buds have had their season, flamed and burnt out in autumn, and have been collected by the brook running beneath them, this brook trout will likely have become an adult, one of November's brilliant breeding males. Most females also mature at the end of their second summer.

I rise and wade into the brook.

Royal fern (Osmunda regalis)

Entering the water constitutes a milestone in the year for me: from now until November I will have this closer contact, this more intimate union with the watery home of the trout I seek. The footing here is solid, and not so slippery as it is along most of the muddy lowland margins. The growth of royal ferns builds up a durable mass that would seem to have the tenure of a boulder at the brook channel's scouring margin. Thaw has had its way, but not so much as a knuckle of uncurling green shows on the mounds. The clear, streaming water of the brook is now 50°F, but the stirring of life proceeds slowly. Not a single fish-shape moves in the water,

Wood turtle (<u>Clemmys insculpta</u>)

so I look to land, searching the slope of the west-facing bank before beginning my ascent. Before I take a step I discover one of my signal signs of spring. Just atop the crest of the high banking, protruding from a drift of leaves that has collected under a ruin of blackberry canes and fallen branches, I detect the serrated edge of a wood turtle's shell. The color and soft dry luster of the shell, and its zigzag margin, are well matched to the leaves and litter into which the turtle has shouldered, leaving most of the surface of her carapace exposed to the warm sunlight. Like the earliest woodland wildflowers this turtle will make use of the abundant sunlight reaching earth before the

trees leaf out. Without getting closer I recognize this one. The points of the ninth and eleventh marginal plates of her carapace have been chipped off as a result of some attack or mishap at some time in her life, a "notching" that allows me to recognize her from season to season. She is one of the wood turtles, some young, some old, who overwinter in Royal Fern Pool. This one has come out of the icy water and ascended this slope to take some of the first sun of her twenty-third spring. How ancient this sculptured turtle seems in comparison with the yearling trout who drifted for some moments in clear water lit by the sun of his second April. This wood turtle has outlived five or six generations of brook trout, and will outlive generations more. I will not disturb her on one of her initial communions with dry earth and warm sun this season. I have checked her closely before, and know the pattern of her plastron and the annual growth rings on its plates, which are still clear enough to give an accounting of her age.

I take in this moment, this turning of another year toward April and renewed life, the early spring sun on this slope of warming earth and in the water flowing below it, this turtle and trout and their world intact. All of this could be lost so easily, this natural construct and its systems and their rhythms. It can be lost as easily as vast expanses of the incomparable and irreplaceable natural world have already been lost to the unchecked spreading-out of the human world and its tragically anthropocentric view of the earth.

In the face of this, the trout go, the turtles go, their very waterways and landscape go. Until recent times, the loss has not been widely reported. Even now, it all too often goes unnoticed or, if is noticed, the loss is either championed or accepted. Native trout and wood turtles are representative of the wildlife that is the first to be edged out of existence as natural habitats are encroached upon, altered, fragmented, or obliterated altogether. So much of the wild earth disappears with a strange quiet. Native brook trout, so quick to take the hook and so limited in habitat, can be fished out in a matter of weeks. Wood turtles are increasingly carried off via incidental collecting, as the eradication and accessing of their historic hideaways exposes them to anglers, canoeists, hikers, and bikers. Ever-expanding networks of increasingly traveled roads are fatal to their populations, and these turtles suffer something of an equivalent to "angler mortality" in being extirpated by professional (generally illegal) collection for the pet trade. Many of the populations of these native animals in their diminished wild places are so limited that the loss of a surprisingly few breeding adults, or the alteration or elimination of a margin of their supporting habitat, can lead to their disappearance. They can vanish in a single season.

But the first stirrings of this spring finds this favorite brook as it has been, year after year. The glimmering presence of the brook trout parr in clear water between riffles and pools, and the enduring wood turtle's still and silent communion with the spring sun attest to the continuance of this wild place. Left alone, it perseveres. I take the brook trout and the wood turtle as my indicator species. If they are here, it is because their habitat has not been subjected to human interference, and remains unbounded and intact, its ecological and spiritual dimensions holding, undiminished, in a sharply narrowing natural world. If they vanish, there will be no good in my coming here. The first walks out in spring can be uneasy ones.

Early Flowering and Leafing Out

*I went out to the hazel wood, • Because a fire was in my
head, • And cut and peeled a hazel wand, • And hooked
a berry to a thread; • And when white moths were on
the wing, • And moth-like stars were flickering out, • I
dropped the berry in a stream • And caught a little silver
trout.*

—William Butler Yeats

Along the Channel in Spring: 19 April

Sun and mild winds, a late afternoon filled
with red-winged blackbird calls that invite
and draw me to the channel below the old
railroad bridge, where it floods through
open country. No forest here, just shimmering acres of alders and willows, sedges and
grasses, a world fully charged with spring
rains and sunlight. The water is high and
swift, the fishing is difficult; but for the trout
the world is as boundless as it will ever be,
and their own territorial options will be
unrestricted for the next two months, until
summer solstice and the ensuing time of low
water. It is all the harder to track these wild
fish at this time of year. From a high knoll I
look down on the sky-reflecting channel
with its quiet, dark swirls. I descend to the
water through a slope thicketed with beaked
hazelnut, whose minute magenta flowers
first graced the gray woods two weeks ago. I
find no earlier flowers, and so seek them
out, as a measure of the progress of each
year's spring. Now, as fully in bloom as they
can be, they must still be looked for, but
once noticed, they ornament the day. Their
male catkins are long tassels now, and I set
pollen clouds loose as I use their slender
stems as handholds in making my way
down the slope. At water's edge, the high-
water mark of spring flood, hazelnut yields
to the wet-footed alders, then to sweetgale
and willow as the floodplain deepens. I set

more pollen adrift on the sweep of wind as I enter the water through strands of emergent sweetgale. In neoprene waders, I make my immersion into the world of the trout.

Like the water, time seems to spread out before me as my wake ripples outward among the alders and willows. Waist-deep, I am still among emergent shrubs. I know these waters well, having familiarized myself with them over previous seasons at shallower times of year. The water is a chill 52°F, wonderful for trout, but a challenge to my insulation and will, though I have waded streams 15° colder. I am reminded of some of the basic differences between the element of trout and my own ambience, one of them being that water conducts away heat twenty-seven times faster than air. And even in this backwater I am aware that water is nearly eight hundred times as dense as air. I would never be able to hold my own out in the current of the channel at this season. In the open flow, I would be swept away, as would the trout themselves. But all along the brook's curling, whirlpooling races lies quieter water, and brook trout could hold along the undercut banks, behind the few boulders of this stretch, downstream of turfy holdfasts, or even in backwater beaver-channel impoundments. There is water within water, and these fish know their water well. I am intrigued with the area around a beaver lodge, where trout are evident in less turbulent times. Curiously, there is a dam, but it is fifty yards or more downstream. The lodge, though surrounded by a moat even in times of low water, seems more like a bank-beaver operation. It has been quite active, in any case, for several years. There is always a great strewing and jamming of many-branched tree lengths in the channel just off the lodge, a perpetually renewed tangle that is not a dam, but has the effect of a screen across the water. Hooded mergansers nest along this channel, and I have seen common mergansers hunt in it, kingfishers survey it from the air, and mink prowl its wetland margins; but for all these predators, trout are here at least for parts of the year and I suspect the branching logjams of the beavers are an important trout hideout.

The trout of this brook are active now, though it would be hard to say exactly where they are. Once the water temperature reaches 50°F or so, their winter-suppressed metabolism picks up, they move out of their overwintering holds, and sharply step up their feeding. Typical of salmonids, brook trout establish hierarchies as they reclaim their feeding stations. In the restless waters of spring, there are skirmishes among the trout, as they settle out a spacing order in the stream. These contests are resolved quickly, and early in the year; the established hierarchy then goes unchallenged throughout the remainder of the season. Trout have to swim against water all of their lives; they cannot afford to exhaust themselves struggling with one another.

One of the problems associated with introducing hatchery fish into streams with native populations is that the residents tend

The channel in spring

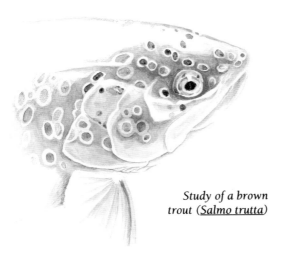

Study of a brown trout (Salmo trutta)

to vigorously oppose the stocked fish, the hierarchy breaks down, and in some cases the introduced fish are chased to death. In other situations, the stocked fish replace the natives. This agonistic behavior, whether within the same species or among different species, is a threat to the survival of all the trout involved.

Under natural conditions, the uncontested established order is based on size. Each trout comes to recognize the others in a stream section, and his or her place within it. By genetic design, the largest fish occupies the best feeding station, and this size-to-favorability ratio prevails on down through the entire population. These positions may be decided by a nose, or by a considerable stretch of water. Should the biggest fish be taken, by a natural predator or by angling, every trout in the pool moves up a notch.

The brook trout of this channel may well overwinter here, and certainly the con-

ditions of this reach in spring and early summer are favorable, but two factors would likely keep them from being year-round residents. One of these is that during most years the water slows to a near stand-still in July and August, and the water level drops notably. The bordering wetlands provide no significant shading canopy, and at low water the channel warms up to levels intolerable for brook trout, who come under stress as the temperature approaches 68°F. With an optimum water temperature of 57°F, this species perishes if constrained to water in the upper 70s. A corollary problem is that warm, slow-flowing, or still water does not hold the oxygen level these fish require. All trout seek cool water, but there are varying tolerances among the species. Rainbow trout can survive exposure to water as warm as 85°F, if it is well oxygenated, but their preferred range is from 65°F to 68°F. Brown trout have a threshold a little over 80°F, but their ideal range is from 65°F to 75°F. Consequently, these two species have been widely stocked in waters that run warmer as a consequence of human activities and are no longer suited for brook trout, who prosper at temperatures between 56°F and 65°F. The second factor that would prevent brook trout from living here year-round is that this reach of the brook lacks the riffled, upwelling gravel sweeps necessary for brook trout spawning. Mature trout must migrate to such locations upstream during their late-autumn breeding season.

Before European settlement and its negative impact on habitat, brook trout were abundant and widespread in a bewildering range of waterways, from tiny, cascading mountain streams to slow-flowing, muck-bottomed meadow brooks. They held forth in ice-water on bedrock, beaver ponds, deep or shallow streams, and rivers. This native northeastern North American trout is in fact an extremely adaptable fish, provided it has access to occasional gravel beds with upwelling water, and cool, well-oxygenated streams. Not much to ask for, and available by the thousands of miles not long ago, but hard to come by now.

Nevertheless, the world into which I wade today appears a perfect one for trout, and I know that they spend at least one season here. In reaches of rivers or streams where all their living and spawning needs are met, brook trout might live out their entire lives along a stretch of a hundred yards or so. Although there is a sea-run form, this species is essentially nonmigratory, in contrast to such salmonids as the restless rainbow trout, who, as they grow larger, move inexorably toward deeper, colder waters, and will end up in a lake, or, in the case of the anadromous steelhead forms, the ocean itself, if any route is open to them.

I wade out toward the main current, with the idea of getting free enough of the interminable branches to work the slower curls and lulls along the shrub margins. From my waist down I am in the world of the trout, while my head and shoulders are brush-ing the realm of the red-winged blackbirds, who take no apparent notice of me as they continually call out, and flash their wings and joust in the tops of the alders. Later in the spring, when they are nesting, my passing here will not go uncontested. Far too short of the channel, I find myself in deep water. The alders are inundated well up their leaning, white-speckled trunks, and the silver-catkinned silky willows I skirt are up to their throats in the clear spring flood. The brook trout's world is brimful; they could swim among branches that will hold blackbird nests in a matter of weeks.

The fishing is hard. It's not just that the widely spread-out, elusive, and extremely alert native trout are hard to catch here, it's that the act of fishing is itself difficult in the thickets of emergent shrubs, underwater tangles, sudden deep-muck regions, and capricious currents that mark the waters of spring. The leafing-out that will make these matters all the more challenging has barely begun. The concept is to try out at least a few patterns, and work some weighted nymphs in the complex depths of the brook. But very few reaches of this

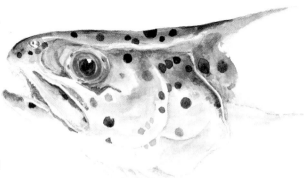

Study of a rainbow trout (<u>Onchorynchus mykiss</u>)

stream allow the working of a fly rod, and possibilities for a spinning reel rarely extend beyond a few feet. A drop or flip of line is all the terrain generally permits. As I cling precariously to slender silky willow branches, edging my way along a deep drop, I remind myself that these arduous environmental barriers, these very physical impediments, keep this a place of solitude, and allow some native trout to continue their existence. A good deal of the habitat along this mile of brook is virtually impenetrable. Its trout are scattered about, wary, and tend to keep to the most hidden recesses. They have other things than fishhooks with which to contend, as mink pace the thicketed banks, mergansers swim the serpentine channels, and kingfishers watch from dead trees and overhangs. These trout have fears more ancient than the tread of a fisherman's boots.

Maybe there are trout here today, maybe not. Perhaps they are still keeping to winter holdouts elsewhere. No trout response has come back to me along my calculated, careful probing runs of line, which, for all the art and patience I could draw from within myself, were forever imitating bird's nests in branches, retrieving beaver sticks, or confusing me with strikes of water and pulls of stone. Per-

Trout lily (<u>Erythronium americanum</u>)

haps the trout are just upstream of where I started fishing, or immediately downstream of my pool of abandonment. As I wade from the cold water, taking great pleasure and a measure of warmth from the last sunlight lingering on the low-lying wetlands, a bittern booms from the neighboring sedge meadow, blackbirds continue calls that have never ceased from the time of my arrival, and spring peepers take up an intensifying chorus that will go on until dawn.

First Warm Rain: 21 April

A trout would have to make quite a wave to reveal his presence today. Heavy rainfall has rendered the brook's surface opaque and unreadable. Larger drops from overhanging trees create widening circles that spread among the countless rings of the raindrops all along the stretch of pools. Swollen buds collect beads of water to shower on me as I brush against brookside red maples and alders, or tunnel my way through the silky dogwood. I am soaked by this rain within a rain. But it is a warm one, the year's first, and not merely warm in contrast with sleet, snowmelt, and ice-water, but warm in itself, on the face, on the wrists.

All is agreeable enough as I leave a temporary shelter in the pines, from which I have found no takers for nymphs dipped and twitched in the brook, and head upstream. The steady showering presages May. I watch it flick the hoods of the jack-in-the-pulpits and set the sprouting woodland grass to dancing. The white flowers of the wood anemone under the alders are closed against the rain, as though gone back into buds again. Their delicate leaves tremble. In the ironwood thicket I see the wet sheen of trout lily leaves, a great carpet of

Red eft (Notophthalmus viridescens)

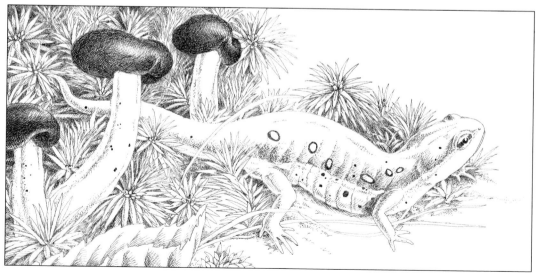

them flickering with a white, almost electric, light. The glistening brightness of their leaves conceals their rusty, mottled patterns. It is a good day for amphibians: I see a red eft wandering this woodland garden.

I set my line free to run in a silver spill and it uncoils to join the brook's swift riffling over gravel and stone. Almost at once the line tightens and is drawn quickly back to the undercut bank. I set the hook and turn the trout, feeling his weighty resistance. Down-and-under, every thrust is down-and-under. I pull up-and-out; the trout and I argue on our respective ends of the line. I see a bronze-and-white flash, one instant only, but vibrant enough to be read in the swirl of darks, lights, and movement. Our duel is one of touch and feel, each of us dealing with a force from an unseen quarter. It matters little that I am rain-blind. I work the trout out of the bankside tangles, into the open surge of the current. I think I see his darkness for a moment among the rings of rain and the ripplings that come and go at the surface. Taking my line in one hand, I slide my rod off to one side and behind me on the bank, and at the brook's edge hand-over-hand the tugging line, pulling the trout up onto the mossy bank. He flips and wriggles wildly among the trout lilies, then lies still for a moment. The season's advent finds an image here, as the brook-glazed trout glows on the rain-wet earth. Air, earth, and water are almost one world today. The ocher-golds of the fish's radiant speckles complement the colors of his namesake flowers. With a sudden thrust he is off the hook, slips through leaves that cup tiny pools of rainwater, swims a body length over saturated moss, and slides off into the water flowing by.

May Day: Meadow Pond and Willow Brook

I walk first along the outlet brook from Meadow Pond, following it upstream from its point of joining Willow Brook, up a white-ash and red-maple bordered stretch and out into the meadow. Here there are open sweeps of reed canary grass interspersed with alder copses, through which twisting channels of clear water run. The trout of this reach keep to undercut banks and overhanging sprays of tussock sedge and reed-grass. Having found no fish along the wooded section of this outlet brook, I will try my luck in the glowing meadow, which is filled with bird calls, from the twitterings and melodies of swamp and song sparrows in the brushier thickets along the waterways, to the ringing cries of red-winged blackbirds from the cattail margins of the pond, and the sweet, piercing calls of meadowlarks, which descend from the tops of high pines at the meadow's edge. This is my English chalk stream, or as close an approximation as I can find among the acidic waters of my particular region. Granite, not trout-favoring limestone, underlies the spongy earth I walk and the clear to tea-colored streams I wade. The brook trout who are the objects of nearly all of my outings are more tolerant of acidic conditions than are rainbow and other stocked species.

The downstream section of the brook this one joins is stocked in the early season, and fished heavily for a time after that. Native trout have been eliminated there, but in more remote and untraversable upper reaches, both of these small streams harbor populations. The degree of wildness, in the landscape and in the trout, increases with the distance from the stocking point. A small population of wood turtles, with which I was familiar over a span of six years, disappeared from the lower, stocked region of Willow Brook over ten years ago, as foot traffic increased tremendously along the streambanks and automobile traffic became much heavier on the nearby, unfortunately stream-paralleling, country road. A casual look at the entire area would give the impression that things have not changed in the past two decades. The purple-fringed orchis that once flowered where the wood turtles roamed have gone the way of the turtles and the native trout. Stocked trout do not linger long after being introduced into a natural waterway. About half of them are generally caught (or "recovered") within a

Marsh marigold (<u>Caltha palustris</u>)

few days. Those hatchery-reared fish that are not immediately hooked in this put-and-take fishing usually do not fare well in the wild, where they are vulnerable to natural predators and ill equipped to shift to natural diet and survival patterns. As few as 5 percent of these planted fish are left at the end of the angling season, and they must face winter and other challenges they are not well suited to survive. There are holdovers, however rare, and in time the wildness comes back into them, the color and wariness, speed and grace of the native speckled trout. On a natural diet, even their pale

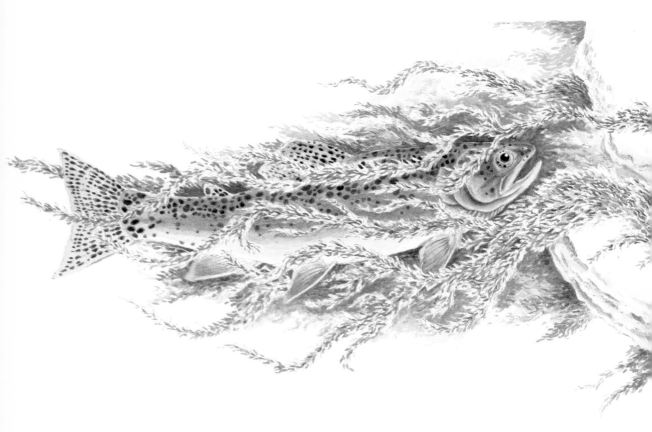

white flesh becomes suffused with the glowing salmon color of a wild brook trout.

Ducking and dodging to keep my shadow off the water, I set on up the outlet brook, at a place between the managed and the wild, where the native and the stocked meet and mingle, and where any trout caught could be a surprise. The bright May morning is not long in fulfilling a fishing promise. I slither into an alder thicket, trying not to rock it on its flooded, sodden moorings, and work to set myself solidly enough among the slender trunks to reach my line out over the racing meadow stream. The current cuts sharply and deeply around mounds of tussock sedge here, and slides beneath undermined holdfasts of reed canary grass, then divides around a tall, midstream hedge of silky willow. My baited hook flashes over the clean-swept sand of a surprisingly deep pool; the brook is little more than two feet wide at this point, but runs more than three feet deep. Back under the water-carved, root-bound earth, my hooked worm finds a taker. There is no reluctance on the part of what is surely a trout. My line is tugged sharply and my rod flinches. There is at least one pole-bender in this lovely little meadow brook. The fish pulls hard, runs deep, and vibrates an intense energy to the hands that work to reel him in before the line is wound around roots and tangles in the stream. As I draw him from the deep-shadowed undercut I see bright, bronze turnings, and flashes of deep red fins. As always, the sharp whites of the leading edges of the fins give form to the trout's acrobatic thrashes in the swirling flow. Drawing him toward me, I see his scattering of brilliant red spots. This one is a native.

With birds singing all around me, I lay the fish, a keeper, on the perfect mound of a tussock sedge at brookside; he is wild and beautiful among the golden-ocher strands of previous seasons' growth, through which are spearing the first gray-green shafts of this year's leaves. The day gleams in his eye.

I move on up to the meadow pond and wade along its shallows to a more open flooring among tufts of soft rush. Here I crouch and prepare my rod, then cast to the outer margin of pussy willow and alder stands across the open water. I am onto a fish in an instant, and think it a trout, but in the second instant become aware of the diminished wildness in the bulldogging of the line. Though it was momentary, the energy and spirit with which the native brook trout opposed his hooking and landing in the narrow run of the outlet brook is vivid in my mind and fingertips. I draw a stocked trout up among the rushes, and after the killing lay it on the grassy bank next to the native. The wild trout, as happens so quickly after death, has faded, and yet he is dazzling compared with his hatchery-reared counterpart. There is no brilliance, no glow or radiance in any of the colors of this fresh-caught fish; a dull, purplish wash lies upon him, whitish, flat, and opaque. There is none of the gold glowing from within, his red spots are fireless flecks, and there is no

Studies of a native
brook trout

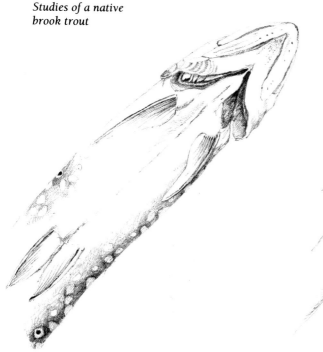

53

Brook trout drifting back behind prey

light in the haloes. When the color goes out of the trout, the wildness goes out of the place, and something of the heart goes out of the fishing.

Without stocking, there would be no brook trout fishing over most of its vast, original range, where it prospered in legendary abundance. The outright loss of habitat over enormous areas and impossible angling pressure eliminated the native populations in short order. One would think a greater lament would have been raised, if not for the splendid animal itself, then for the incomparable waterways in which it ranged. But the loss of natural habitats seemed acceptable, or inev-itable, to the prevailing thinking and attitudes of colonial expansion, and that mentality prevails to the present. Efforts are being made to preserve some few heritage strains of native brook trout that have escaped extirpation, or tragic devaluation by endless genetic interferences and experimentations; most of them poorly thought out, if thought out at all. And if some fish are saved, or come back somehow, where are they to live? The dwelling-place must be as wild and natural as the native trout themselves, and such a place is not commonly to be found in eastern North America, if it is to be found anywhere.

The two fish I kneel before on this greening May Day bank are a sharp reminder of the rare edge I walk and wade, of the good, but sad, fortune I have, with one foot in the lost or altered world and one foot in the wild. There was a time when the balance was there for the making. The beautiful city, the world left alone; the latter has been overrun, and the former is a broken dream. I look upstream, beyond the pond and its beckoning meadow, to the alder tangles, one of the living screens through which I can pass at times and leave so much behind; the living thickets that, for now, screen out enough intrusions to allow native brook trout to flash through sun-slants in perfect springtime water.

Deciding not to get in the way of any more natives on this day, in this brook, I turn back downstream, and take a trout in a lovely pool overhung with silky dogwood. Then I set my rod aside for a time and walk upstream, where things get wilder. Dense brush crowds the water, and the only stream management is done by beavers. Mink come here, and as the brook slants well away from the road and into the hills I'm sure even wilder things drink the water. My own quest for greater taste of the wild leads me up a moss-rock slope laced with rivulets and trickles. Above these I come to a well-remembered seep, where the slope levels out. My timing is correct: the swath of this springtime water-run is lined with the brilliant green leaves of marsh marigolds, many with bright yellow buds and a shiny-petalled first flower or two. To be more precise, it is their timing that is correct. Before the alder canopy can open leaves over the mucky seep, or taller trees on the higher ground lining it can shade this perpetually moist trough above the brook, the marsh marigolds burst into leaf, and flower. In a month or two the sensitive ferns just now trying the milder air above the water-sheets and sodden earth will be waist high to me, completely overshadowing everything beneath them in the shade of the alders. In this late-season world of shade upon shade, wood frogs, peepfrogs, and mosquitoes will be plentiful, but not a trace of the marsh marigolds will be found. For this brief blooming, the long stretch of the seep is theirs. I admire the first flowers, but I am after a salad, not a bouquet, and set to work picking leaves, one or two from this plant, one or two from that. From my earliest trout-times, a tradition of mine has been to provide a dinner of trout and marsh marigold leaves. I have alternately read that the leaves of this plant are an esteemed wild edible and that they are poisonous. In any case, one steamed mess of them each spring has proven a delicious tonic rather than a lethal dose. Another plant asserts itself in this garden of mud, and it, too, is apparently an edible of sorts. There are scattered stalks of cow-parsley, which, if they were to go on and achieve their full potential height of ten feet, would seem to threaten the alders here. This plant was part of the Native Americans' herbal, and is considered an emergency food. With a couple of trout and a bagful of marsh marigold leaves, I will not be needing emergency food tonight. I join the brook again and head back downstream, to see if I can ensure that there will be enough fish to accompany the dinner greens.

The meadow is filled with glimmering wings, and I see spreading rings of silver on the dark, pine-reflecting surface of the pond. My late-afternoon return to Meadow Pond is well timed, my moment coinciding with the thousand-winged moment of these dancers in the still May air. They gleam in the sun as they rise and fall, but they will not be dancing as tonight's moon glimmers on their fallen wings floating on the pond or lying scattered among the sedges and rushes. This is their second journey into the air and, as brief as it is, it will be their longest. From beneath the water the nymphs have ascended, in a living tide, from their half-year to two-year life (I do not know which of the countless mayfly species these are) among the substrate stones, litter, and plants of the pond and its brook, ascended with a like mind at a shared time, to the tension line between the two worlds of water and air. At this thin veil they have become transformed from aquatic burrowers, crawlers, or swimmers to fliers of thin air. For a time on the floating world of the water surface the subimagoes, or duns, ride currents or sail in light breezes over the pond, on papery vessels that are the skins of their former lives, after splitting them down the back and emerging, winged, on the edge of a new, transitory existence. How are these new moments measured, as dun-colored wings are quickly dried, temporary wings serving only to carry them to shore, in flights of seconds or minutes, over distances of feet or

Ephemeroptera. In this ascendant, transcendent moment of the mayflies' mating, I do not exist. They rise and fall all about me, brush wings on my face, come to ruin against my vest, rest briefly on my walking stick.

These are the long-lived ones, the creatures of half a day or, at outer limits, two days, who were not cut off just before they reached the surface, or seized upon the water before their first unfolded wings could take to air. These are not the ones whose journeys ended on that initial flight to a staging area for the fragile-winged mating dance. My coming here has been fortuitous, my timing chance. But the trout in the water and the swallows in the air have had it timed from the outset, preceded by an anticipation leaving little to chance. The first nymph to rise into the light-filled water did not go unnoticed. Nor did the first dun, drifting and drying its wings. Now the winging ones are well attended. These mayflies are intent, not mindless, but they must be oblivious to everything around them. In mild May air they do a dance choreographed long ago, a dance of minutes that is ancient. Out of this, masses of eggs, the source of the next generation of dancers, will be entrusted to the water's keeping.

Some trout sip, some break the placid surface. I see the rings of their rises. Occasionally there is a splashing leap. I enter the shallow margin among the rushes,

yards? Life is a matter of hours now, but perhaps these flights seem endless. A myriad of them land among the reed canary grass, the sedges and alders. Here a second transformation takes place, a second shedding leaving behind another life-encasement. Now, as imagoes, the mayflies travel higher yet on glistening wings; two sets of wings for an aerial life of hours. This final flight, this last ascension, is ephemeral; but who can measure the journey, in mayfly terms, from the bottom of the stream or pond to the surface, then to the nearby shore, and finally into the air? Water, earth, and air; they have a different form for each, and perhaps they receive a touch of fire as sunlight plays on their glimmering wings. This element-encompassing journey finds its place in time in a manner for which we have no equivalent; we attempt a definition in naming the entire order of these insects my wide-spreading ripples quieting the fish and giving spent and struggling mayflies a last ride on the water. I wade up the inlet brook to where cattail and bulrush give way to alder and silky dogwood, then leave the water and steal along the northside bank, keeping my shadow off the brook. The lowering sun lights up the west-running brook from behind me. This is the time of day to search this stretch of water, this time of year. In any open space over the water, any clearing among the alders, mayflies dance. Fallen ones spin slowly along on the drift.

I hear a fish working the surface, and stop. Mayflies rest on my shoulder, on my left hand holding onto a steadying alder, and on my right hand gripping my walking stick. I hear another fish swirl, not far ahead, a brook trout I am sure, in a deep pool below a tall upreach of peachleaf willow. Advancing slowly, I see the next rippling. I inch forward, keep still in the screening alders, and look for the shape of a fish. In the backlit pool, I see the brook trout shadow a mayfly. He has come out from under the willow embankment and taken up a foraging station behind a large rock that trails fountain moss over clean-swept sand. I treasure this pool in any season, and all the more when it holds a native trout. The drift comes to him perfectly, and though this is a shrub-shrouded brook, I am sure the current has presented him mayflies all afternoon.

Brook trout leaping for mayflies

Swirling water, undulating fountain moss, wavering shadows from streamside stems, here the vermiculate-patterned back of the trout dissolves and disappears without his moving, even as I look down on him. He slips back in the water, falls back with its drift, at the same speed. With no perceptible

action he adjusts the angle of his pectoral fins, directing the current under them at a slant, so that the stream carries him with it, downstream and toward the surface at the same time. This deft maneuver is timed with the drift of the mayfly trapped on the surface, and as the trout elevates in the water he is able to inspect his potential food, effortlessly riding backward in the water, his nose just downstream of his prey, which is beyond protesting. His decision made, the trout intercepts the insect with a quick, arching roll on his side, the bronze-and-white belly-flash electrifying me, as litle as I am able to see of it. The trout immediately straightens, head-down in the water, having barely dimpled the surface. As the slight rings of his taking dissolve in the moving stream, he faces into the flow, a simple

reversal of his fins allowing him to slice into the current and be driven to the bottom. Once there, he makes his first movements since his sighting of the mayfly, and glides upstream along the much slower current immediately above the brook's bed, to take up his original lie. By such grace and economy of means trout sustain themselves in a medium that is forcefully resistant even when it is not in motion, and that often runs counter to them. They have perfected a martial art in which opposing force is turned into their own strength.

Fishing for Natives: 15 June

The sky is deep, and clear blue. The day is cool, not much above 60°F; trees are rock-

ing in blustery northwest winds. June's new growth glistens with the reflected light of this dazzling day.

Fishing for natives, I travel far to the north, where wild brooks and their wild trout are, for now, as they were when I first went fishing, and I can fish as I did then. I thread my way through willows and dogwood (the light is like water on them), into the marshy meadows of a series of beaver dams. I regret how easily a path becomes worn in the grasses and sedges, in the yielding earth of the marshy banks, and make a wide circle of the flowering blue flag and forget-me-not. I try not to injure the plants, or leave a record of my passing.

Nervous red-winged blackbirds cluck to one another with worried, raspy whispers as I wade past their nests in the sweetgale. The great drift of mid-June's white-pine pollen lies in a sulphur-yellow dust on amber and black water. There is the ancient anxiousness as I approach open water; the desire for stealth that makes stealth almost impossible, as I fumble with rod, reel, and line. A capricious wind works against the light line and nearly weightless worm, a constant interference with the delicate maneuverings of the bait among the tangles of overhanging alders and buttonbush, toward shadows that might harbor trout. There is a shadowy movement in the water as the bait is struck swiftly. For an instant the fish is visible as he seizes the worm with bulldog shakings, and then with a rapid run of line the trout again becomes part of the water. I set the hook and pull the

fish to an earth it resists, thrusts against violently, as it is landed.

Carmine spots, encircled with violet blue, line the olive-and-gold body, slashes of red-orange flare on the fins; a darker red runs from the gills. I complete the necessary life-taking, twisting the fish's head back. The message of death is telegraphed along the liquid spine, and in a shivering instant the creature slides like quicksilver from my hands and lies shimmering on the earth. The light of air, not water, is reflected in a gold-rimmed eye.

An oriole flashes among the alders, a jewel set in a vast gray-and-green tapestry, as the trout, invisible to me in the water, are jewels set in a great amber-and-bronze expanse. I take advantage of the wind-riffled opacity of the surface to wade slowly, heron-like, to a deeper pool. Behind me the beaver dam's entire length is lined with glowing rust-orange pine needles, lined as carefully as any bird's nest, by the wind and water.

My line tenses, slackens. I come alert, only to realize that this is the fifth trout, the limit. In that same instant I am filled with regret, a sense of loss, that there is a limit, a limit on trout, on beaver dams and waterways, on open spaces and afternoons...a limit on time itself.

Solstice: Time of Low Water

Things that pass us, go somewhere else and don't come back, seem to communicate directly with the soul. • That the fisherman plies his craft on the surface of such a thing possibly accounts for his contemplative nature.

—*Thomas McGuane*

Morning at the Beaver Lodge: 17 June

The wild, swirling waters of late March have dropped away, but spring rains have kept the wetlands charged, and even as the turning of the season draws close, the channel has a drift. I walk a wet alder woods, then enter the brook through a deep beaver sluiceway. Though the water drops away noticeably on

the threshold of summer, and in smaller streams I can resort to my hip waders, I require my chest-high neoprene waders

here. I have rolled them down to my waist. I wade from the east, the morning sun behind me. I will hide myself and my shadows as best I can among the alders and their shadows.

I stop near a high boulder and run a line around the giant rock, trying the surface and the depths. I always drop a hook first at my feet, in case I have moved slowly enough and been disguised enough among the plays of water and shadow to go unnoticed. Rarely do I catch a fish on such an initial test of the water, but, if the place is right and the time is right, a trout could as well be under one's feet as under an opposite bank. No fish…but at least there is a clear stretch here, and I am not hung up. I settle into my niche, cranberries flowering at my elbow, flanked by alders, wedging myself against the cushion of growth that rests on solid rock. It is a good place to view the morning and the brook. A beaver glides by. Mosquitoes have dropped away with the day's advance, and the blackflies seem not so bad along the water margin, or perhaps I am at last becoming somewhat inured to them. In wooded sections, they are death. The beaver's widening wake reaches me in my half-hideaway. He either did not see me, or did not care, and kept to the surface as he passed by, perhaps as grateful for the sweet air of a June morning and the sun in his face as I am as I turn my head to watch his upstream progress. He does not call at the lodge. He could be the member of another tribe, or on some pressing errand. But he or some other beavers have been proverbially busy in the channel off the lodge, as great masses of fresh-cut branches reach out of the water, some of them aspen fluttering leaves so fresh and green they must have been cut last night or at dawn. No beavers move in the steady slide of water, but some fish-neighbors swirl and dimple the surface from time to time. They keep close to the sheltering margin of the endless vegetation, and the impossible brush-piles of the beavers. Here there is food and cover for

Studies of native brook trout

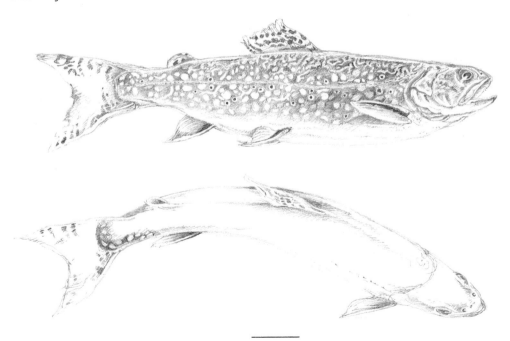

beaver and trout alike. Phoebes flit from alders to take insects over the water and from the beaver-cut branches. The air is theirs, the water belongs to the trout, and they both work the thin membrane dividing water and air. Red-winged blackbirds confine their clatter primarily to the shrub margins, but they, too, flash and preen, argue and look for food in the beaver's woodlot. Hunters who are hunted, dragonflies need all their aerial dexterity as they dodge birds and pick off smaller insects among the midstream branches. Just how risky this business is for them is attested to by the piles of glittering wings beneath the phoebe's feeding perch and the scatterings of them in the sweetgale near the redwings' nests.

And trout I cannot see are doubtless lively in the extensive underwater stores of stems and branches, which attract aquatic and terrestrial insects, to complement the drift of things brought along by the current. On the surface of things (literally and figuratively), this would seem an enticing trout lie, with food or protection available at the flick of a tail, and water aerated enough, deep enough, cool enough, and forever moving by. This is a moment, as everything seems a moment in the stream of one thing or another, be it in a brook, a season, a life, or time itself; that all things are intimately connected, if they are not, in fact, one and the same. This is a moment for trout that is close to the perfect trout dream. At this point in their life, and in the life of the stream and of the season, the flow is favorable. The water's depth, temperature, and

dissolved oxygen content are within peak parameters, and satisfaction for their one earthly desire at this stage of the year—something to eat—is immediately available, with abundance and variety at every hand. Trout, like dragonflies and fishermen, lead mortal lives. Mink move along the waterways, kingfishers know the channel well, and a man with a hook and line leans against a stone, waist-deep in the water. But given the constant of death, which is linked with life as trout are bound with water, and is an equalizing factor for the salamander under the stone and the eagle among the clouds, this June morning in the brook, poised between the spring floods and the summer droughts, is ideal for trout. At 61°F, the water temperature is well below the summer range of 68°F–72°F that will bring an invasion of warm-water fish, such as fallfish and creek chubsuckers, to this channel.

Fishing just far enough out from the edge of this wetland mélange, and edging my line around and over surface and submerged beaver slash, I might well tempt a brook trout to make that dash from cover, strike, and wheel back down into the deep, dark water and its safeguarding tangles. I count on the legendary readiness of the brook trout to feed, as I do always in my excursions after these natives, so wild and widely scattered. The trick, and the joy, is in the finding of them, and getting some kind of fishing line within their reach without alerting them to take to unreachable, non-feeding cover for an hour or two. Far and away, most of my brook trout sightings are of where they were, a swirl of water and a quickly disappearing surge on the surface. In luckier moments I glimpse a tail, or catch sight of the sharp, white edge of a fin, or see a shadow-shape that can only be that of one of these fish. I'd have to be an osprey, high above, or a merganser deep within the water to see a trout in the channel today. Low to the swirling water, I can see into it only here and there, and generally at close range, even though I keep the climbing sun at the most propitious angle over my shoulder. To see a trout, to know that one is here, I will have to hook one, though I am rather certain of the origin of some of the rings and rises I have seen.

The first casts are all snags, some of them on my own side of the brook. I reel in a length of aspen, which zigzags in the trick-mirror water like slow, green-gold lightning. As I extract my hook, I admire the tooth-work of the beaver who debarked this branch, then let it flow away out of sight downstream. Suddenly, I am onto a fish. Out of my absorption in the day, my immersion in its chilling water, my mental drifting away on its warming air, my blind and nearly unconscious workings with rod and line and constant eye-search of the mesmerizing water, an electrifying series of surges from my line brings an instant focus. I forget sometimes that I am fishing. The fish

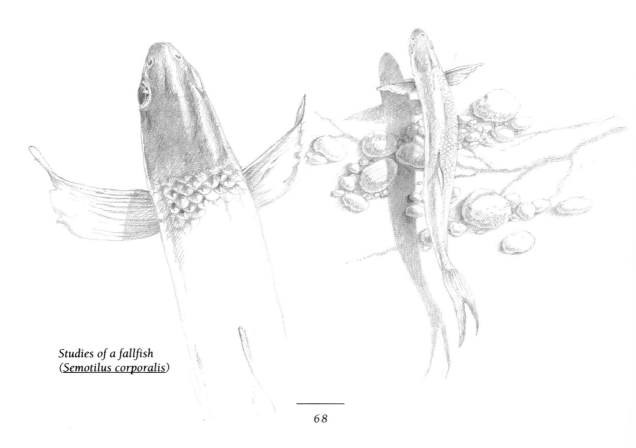

Studies of a fallfish
(*Semotilus corporalis*)

68

thought he was feeding. We are suddenly brought to our respective senses. There is a life at both ends of the line, and immediately each sets to work at its opposing purpose. And then the fish is gone. The line lies slack in the water, its vibrant tension replaced by an emptiness, a lifelessness, as it comes back as a weightless, spiraling thread in the water. The hook, so quick to take in my own vest, an alder leaf, a beaver stick; so quick to set and hold unyieldingly in stone-hard, water-logged wood, cannot find a hold in the soft, thin-boned mouth of a fish. I think, sometimes, as I use my lips to hold a hook for a moment, or move one close to my mouth as I bite off a trailing bit of line, of how swiftly, unforgivingly, and painfully that tiny sharp point with its ensnaring barb could take its hold. It seems at times the trout take their food with the lightest kiss.

Summer Solstice: 21 June, late afternoon

I keep a vigil at the bridge. One of those four turnings of the year I cannot help but mark. It will be a while yet before I really perceive that the days, which have been growing longer since a point in time late in March, an impression that for a time tricks me every year into believing that there will be no turning back, will now shift and run in the other direction, with a daily accruing of darkness. I would not notice, until I saw something in the plants, a ripening of the sedges or bronzing in the burreed reflected on the water, or noted the appearance of the swamp milkweed flowers or realized that the last of the swamp roses were scattering their petals on the water. Perhaps the length of my shadow on the open ground would startle me at a certain afternoon hour one day as I came up out of the dusky margins of a wooded brook. But each of the things living in and along the streams has its own close reckoning, its measuring and timing of each moment of each season's progress. Their calendars are in their structure, and possess a precision I cannot imagine.

A marking on a page of numbers brings me here, to keep the final hours of daylight and see the darkness come on. The brook is nearly still, but trout are here. Or, at least, a trout is here. From my stand in a screen of alders I look upstream in time to see a splendid brook trout enter a shaft of light from the lowering sun. The perfect trout-form lights up in the water, its countless speckles gleaming. A speckled trout indeed, with flecks of gold, and those scattered spots of fiery red. Leisurely in the water, drifting like some dream-fish, the trout ascends without apparent movement and hovers, lingering in the spotlight. He then glides to the base of a great trussock-sedge mound at the edge of the pool's deep drop. Just beneath the surface the trout becomes completely motionless against the amber backdrop of the sedge's skirts of past seasons' growth. The trout is still. No caddis larva moves in the tussock strands, no nymph breaks for the surface, no moth flutters out from the weedy shore to become ensnared on the water. For a moment the trout is suspended, out from any cover, removed from any line of drift. Then he is gone. His brilliance disappears in darkness.

I cross the bridge, skirt marshy backwaters and red maple swamps, and walk the brook's wooded run. It is dark when I come out. In less than starlight, the logging road I walk is barely visible. A wind comes up, so slight it barely seems to move along the dirt road's narrow corridor. Along its leafy edges nothing moves. It is a whisper of a nightwind that keeps to open courses, the deer paths, logging road, and brook itself, for it requires no solid footing. I stop at the base of a high, domed knoll rising abruptly on the eastern bank, above the bridge. I am held in place as a different wind swirls up around me, earth-warm, circling the outcropping boulders and soughing in the lower branches of the tall white pines. Here is a dialogue, another of those I encounter in my trout-wadings or trout-walks. Nightwind, stone, and tree, conversant in the darkness, with the darkness. In a sky-space close to the trunk of one of the imposing trees, a tiny star appears. I see no other points of light in openings among the branches, or in the sky above the little clearing in which I stand. Clouds have closed in. The wind has different voices, barely audible, in the nearby hazelnut thicket, in the pines towering above it, and in the bracken in the clearing. I haven't the ears to hear its sound on stone. I cannot name the star, or know what distance in time and space it measures, but I think of Stonehenge, that at this time next year, at summer solstice, this same star will be held in this same sky-space among these pines. If there is a Druid place anywhere among the brooks and river-stretches I wander, it is here.

I walk on out and cross the bridge. Not a breath of air moves against my face in this open place, not a tremble of wind is raised on the still water that finds a light in the darkness. Wind-voices from the knoll behind me fade in darkness and very little distance.

Trout-Seekers: 29 June

Shortly after dawn, as I approach the channel, a great blue heron rises from the pool above the bridge. As my eyes are almost always on the near water at my approach, I seldom see these birds before they see me, and my typical first sighting is of a great, silent shadow, not quite blue, not quite gray, separating itself from the landscape and ascending with impossible slowness, becoming a wide-winged bird as it levels off and moves apart. On one occasion when I saw the heron before being seen, as I made my way through dense hemlocks at the headwaters of a small northern river, I froze in my tracks and waited and watched. Leaving an open pool to the one who was there first, I learned something of what time is to a heron. Her hunting pool was more of a little pond, an opening in dense conifers where water lingered in a sedgy bowl thicketed with winterberry holly before taking up a rushing-stream pace through a narrow outlet and flowing along a gradual, rock-studded descent. I'm not sure if the heron was fishing or frogging; I doubt it mattered to her whether her breakfast had fins or legs. It was excruciating to match her holding-still. I was determined to wait her out, though I was somewhat anxious to try the pool's deeper pockets for trout. Long minutes were followed by interminable minutes. The heron rotated her head and long, spearlike bill with such a slight gesture she seemed to disappear, and I worked to redefine her as I stared fixedly from the hemlock shade. How many trout would I see (or catch), if that were the day's intent, if I could take on a heron's stillness and invisibility? At great length, two measured strides, one foot lifted so slowly its motion was barely detectable; a lifting and closing of the long toes, a reaching forth, a settling into water, toes spreading beneath the surface in their stealthy reach for the bottom. I could not detect a ripple. I expected a lightning-strike of that great bill at any instant. But another stationary pose, this one revealing the intentness of the hunter's black eyes set in burning gold. As the next interminable period of motionlessness began, I considered the heron's situation, the fact that her apparent patience was not without limit. I had caught several fish, but even if I hadn't, a supper awaited me at day's end. Perhaps this lean one had not eaten yesterday. There was no guarantee she'd eat today. Perhaps she still had young to feed. The necessary patience of a heron is set within harsh limitations. If nothing were to be caught here, the next hunting ground might involve a flight of miles. She might have to cross or circle a mountain. Time spent in one place is always measured by hunger. How long to keep still, how long to stay in this tiny eye of water in a great forested landscape, where to go next? As I explored the bird's possible reckonings she lifted off, long legs trailing water, and winged away over the hemlocks. Inevitably, as I fished the pool, I wondered who needed the trout the most, the heron, the pool itself, or me? One would like to imagine trout abundant enough for all needs and desirings; such a time may well have existed. Though I possessed means a heron could never dream of, and did not have to look my quarry in the eye, much less take him with my teeth or fingers, I had no more success than she. If there were trout in the pool at that time, the water kept them.

This early morning's heron is hardly out of sight when I see surgings in the water, against the west bank of the brook and among the dense buttonbush at its margin. I expect a beaver (though this is more a muskrat place) as I watch the disturbance subside, then swirl up anew. It is nothing on the surface, but something very active within the still water. A bird appears. Her sleek back sheds water, the crest of her rust-red head is disheveled from her immersion. How wild she looks, this common merganser, up from the deepest parts of the brook, wide-eyed, spraying water, her stiletto beak poised parallel to the surface. She

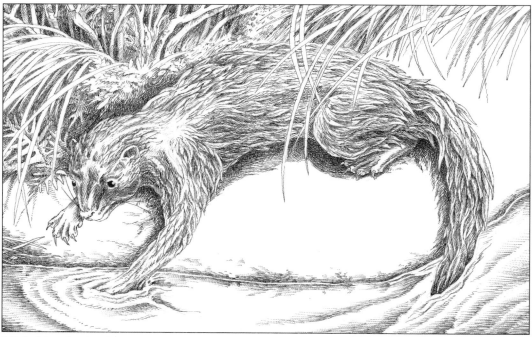

Mink (<u>Mustela vison</u>)

offers little in the way of bird-watching. Her disappearance, quite in contrast with the heron's deliberate leave-taking, is instantaneous. I watch, fully expecting to see a surfacing somewhere along this extensive reach of open water, but I never see her again. This fish-eater swims like a fish, and could be anywhere.

Two days ago, farther downstream, I watched a mink. Spiked and shaggy-looking, as though in midshake after an underwater swim, he rose up above his muddy surroundings, frozen in place for a moment, then took up his furtive slipping in and out of the brook. Dark and wet, he slid eel-like among the tangles, as though he could swim through water or vegetation with equal ease.

His keen eyes were riveted on the water and its margins. Then he doubled back in silence among the shadows from which he had just emerged, though I found it difficult to imagine he had missed anything there.

These encounters with other potential trout-seekers make me all the more aware of the lowering, warming waters. It has been dry; the brook can barely be said to run here, as it essentially stands and waits for the next recharging rains, which may not come until autumn. The steady outflow and evaporation, and the tremendous uptake by the plants living within and lining its every trace have depleted the brook beyond any compensation the scant summer rains have been able to offer. Trout become more vulnerable now, as their world shrinks around them, and their critical thresholds of temperature and dissolved oxygen are pressed.

With images of heron and merganser fresh in my mind, and a clear vision of the rapacious mink, I might fear that the native trout of this brook could not endure. But here, of course, they are in their element. Predation is a normal factor in any natural system, and at times it can be a limiting one. Predators will target concentrations of prey, as the trout themselves rise to mayfly hatches; but when any such densities drop away to the lower levels, they move on, seeking other opportunities. With fish-eaters, favored prey become the more abundant, slower, easier-to-catch species such as shiners and suckers, and even trout competitors like yellow perch. Removal of trout predators from an intact natural system would not lead to a proliferation of trout, as other natural limitations would set in and maintain the numbers the habitat has the capacity to sustain. If one reads the accounts of the extraordinary abundance of brook trout found throughout their range at the time of the arrival of the first colonists, when predators certainly had their greatest numbers and most extensive territory, one must conclude that the trout's troubles do not lie with mink or otters, eagles or osprey. It should not be so easily forgotten how successful brook trout and so many other living things were, until their existence was completely upended by the human activities of the past two hundred years.

Fishing takes a heavy toll on trout. In some waters it is the most signficant factor in the loss of trout, particularly the older and larger individuals within a population. The hook, in its endless themes and variations, is an indiscriminate taker of these fish. Unlike natural predators, it does not select for the weak, the slow, the injured. It takes all comers, and the hand and mind guiding it strive to catch the biggest and best. Trout native to an intact wild environment have a good survival rate against natural predation once they survive the risk-laden journey to maturity. Those who reach reproductive age have more than good luck going for them. Dodging an osprey or outmaneuvering an otter is one thing, avoiding the hook concealed within or masterfully disguised as food is quite another. And this is not to take into account the tremendous devastation of the trout's very world by the inventor of the fishhook, a presumptuous species that sees no conflict in damming and degrading streams and rivers while calling for the elimination of the predators who take a few of "their" trout.

It is apt, as I think of trout-seekers, that a kingfisher's call should rattle out over the stream before me. I see large fish move in the channel, low in its deeper recesses. They are (either) white suckers or creek chubsuckers, I am sure. The water temperature is nearly 70°F here, and warming to their liking. A young pickerel is poised like a lance in a tangle of twigs at water's edge. Trout may yet feed here at dawn, in the cooler shadows, but by now most have shifted to deeper pockets off the beaver

lodge, or the heavily shaded alder sections down the brook. Others may be in the riffled runs beyond the wet meadows, where the brook becomes a wooded stream once more. It is likely the dispersal has included migrations upstream, to runs and deeper pools among alders and red maples, where plunges and tumbles of water are not exactly waterfalls, but enough to aerate the tree-shaded current. This brook, which is remarkably free of human disturbance and management, has a thousand aspects, and the native trout who live here know them all. These speckled fish find places to ride out the hostile winter and perilous scour of thaw, they find springs and seeps and hidden deep pools in the time of low water, and they know the gravel runs with upwelling water in which they can spawn in the near-freezing water of late autumn. These swift and cunning trout are equal to the demands of swimming the waters in which mink and mergansers hunt, and along whose tree-lined stretches kingfishers perch throughout much of the year. When conditions in favored lies turn to the advantage of these trout-hunters, the trout know where to take refuge all along the brook's endlessly varied course. They live here, they have lived in such places for millennia. In such lingering streams of wildness they flare their crimson, white-edged fins and flash their bronzed, gold-speckled sides, vibrantly keeping their time-honored place.

Rainbow trout in plunge-pool

Late July Rain: 27 July

Steady rain becomes heavy as I approach Deer Brook through the dim green light of the alder groves. This is my second good soaking in a week, but in the time of low water even this deluge does not show up in the brook. The thirsty plants and the earth itself slake themselves first, and there is no runoff, no collecting of water save in the most impermeable bowls of rock or hard-packed clay. The brook is lower than I thought it would be; it does not seem there would be any use in fishing even the most propitious pools. But there are holes and cuts along these vegetated, amorphous banks, and a trout or two may hold here, even as August approaches. Wet as a mink I fish the nearly still channel above the old railroad bridge, where the rain and the darkness of the day seem to bind earth and sky together, closing the world in. Green growth all around me, with a sheen of rain, gives off a light of its own, a green-gray light in the space between the black water and the glowering sky.

Rain is pouring on me as I stand beneath a red maple big enough to allow me to straighten up while keeping myself concealed among its lower branches and leaves. A kingfisher drops suddenly from the sky, landing in a dead elm directly across the brook, and not much above my head. Perhaps her low perch indicates that this is not a day suited for high-diving. It must be difficult for her to see into the water at all. I get a good look at her large, rain-ruffled head and sodden crest, and hear her rattling calls loudly and clearly. Maybe she wants to startle some fish into revealing movements, the way a sharply hooting owl sets mice scampering. If this one whose life depends upon it fishes here, perhaps it is worth my while. I take a clue from her, and after her raucous departure try the alder and willow border

Brook trout and northern water thrush (<u>Seiurus noveboracensis</u>*)*

skirting her abandoned fishing-perch. My rain gear notwithstanding, I am soaked; half of me submersed in the world of the trout, half immersed in falling rain.

Stranded Brook Trout: Mid-August

Wood thrush calls drift back and forth across the shaded brook, one seeming the echo of another, weaving the shadows with sound. This mellifluous singing is interspersed with the ringing calls of a northern water thrush. Low water murmurs over stone. I leave the main stream and walk the wet cobble of an ephemeral spring brook, now a trickle disappearing among cool, water-smoothed stones. I lift several rocks and set them carefully back in place. Wriggling larvae live on their wet undersurfaces

and in water-filled gravel beneath them. Many stream invertebrates live a yard or two beneath the rocks and gravel of a stream bottom, where they are safe from trout in times of flow, and unaffected by the emptying of the stream in times of drought. No trout can descend from overhead now, tail-up, nosing stones and stirring gravel to dislodge them, nor is the water layer apt to drop much lower here and desert them, as a seep maintains a steady drift through gravel. Under one of the larger black stones I find a northern two-lined salamander, slender, sinuous, curled into a motionless living arabesque in a watery hollow. Astonished into frozen stillness for a moment upon having the roof of his world removed, he appears a living script in glistening sand, a bold line of speckled bronze, edged with slender black tracings on either side. When movement is recovered, it is swift and serpentine. I wet my hands quickly in the salamander's hollow, as I would wet them before touching a trout, and capture him. The wetness in the sand feels very cold, even in contrast with shaded stones. Once I have

Northern two-lined salamander
(*Eurycea bilineata*)

returned his sheltering rock to its former place in the brook-floor's mosaic, I set the salamander at its lower edge. Some head for daylight, others head for darkness: this lively brookside creature of darkness at once perceives a crevice among the rounded pebbles and slips back beneath his stone.

I walk in the brook's shadowy coolness over its stone or mud bottom and its intermittent bowls of water, trickles, and seeps. A few strides up the slope from this narrow trace the woodland shadows are hot and humid; out on the open marsh and fields the day simmers. Green frogs take to the ferns that line the banks as I wade an ankle-deep pool. A school of blacknosed dace crowds under a stone ledge. Off to one side, in an isolated outreach of this seasonal brook, something surges in the leaf-strewn water. A trout? No other denizen of the brook would explode with such speed and strength, and take such a darting, zigzag course in the shallow water. But this swift and apparently strong one seems to have tunneled into the sunken leaves in this fern-surrounded pool, burrowing more like a frog than a fish. I stir gently with a branch. Another sudden burst of speed, a frantic course in water and leaves, and a hiding. I cannot see this stranded creature, but it must be a fish and surely a trout, a fairly sizable one at that. The movements are so swift that I cannot glimpse their originator as he streaks among sunken leaves. I begin to circle the tiny pool. The fish is off again; apparently he can see me. This rush brings him to an edge so shallow his back and dorsal fin break the surface for a moment, sharklike. Then he is off in the severely limited depths once more. This is indeed a brook trout, and I would have to think he has been isolated for some time. I marvel that no raccoon has detected him, as the tracks of these predators decorate every muddy stretch along and in the brook. Perhaps he has survived by his burrowing strategy, something young trout will resort to in full streams, and which even larger trout have been known to do to escape a predator or to ambush prey. It seems curious that such a mature fish—he must be seven or eight inches long—could have become trapped as this tributary shrank away with the heat and drought following summer solstice. I am reluctant to terrorize him further, but his future here is bleak. If a raccoon does not find him, he will run out of water soon enough, or run out of tolerable temperatures and oxygen levels. I try to crowd him into the shallowest part of the pool, but he flashes by me, and the chase is on. How can anything catch a trout in open water? The trout is valiant as I play him not with a rod and line, but with shadow-gestures, foot-sloshes, and branch-stirrings. I hope to tire the trout before I frighten him to death. It becomes a game of tag I lose at every turn. I never see my quarry, with mud riled up and sodden leaves everywhere in the water. I detect only where he was, his sharp and sudden movements, and, when he is still, a general notion of where he might be. I corral him once more time in the slippery shallows. As exhaustion overtakes him, I make a lunge and scoop through the water, dropping down on my knees. If trout are the picture of grace, I am the embodiment of awkwardness; but I have a living, writhing fish in the collection of mud and leaves I gather into my hands. His wriggling thrusts die away, his gills work frantically. I peel a leaf away from his mud-plastered body and marvel a moment at those radiant colors and patterns one so rarely gets to see. The wet leaves will protect him for a time, but he is impossibly slippery, and if I drop him on my hurried route back to the main brook, he'll not survive.

"You are a keeper," I whisper to the trout cradled in my mucky hands, "but it is the brook that will keep you." His eyes reflect the fern's green glow. I struggle to my feet and race down the brook's path, ignoring the hazards of wet sneakers on wet stones. More quickly than I would have thought possible I am in the stream, trailing clouds of mud in clear water. I wade rapidly to a shimmering pool, glowing amber in a sun-slant among shadow-blue stones and shadow-green leaves. Settling onto my knees on the rock-strewn bottom, I extend my cupped hands into the water, and slowly open them. Leaves and mud swirl outward and begin a drift to the bottom of the pool. My heart sinks as I see the trout motionless in the pool, on one side, his rippled green-gold and umber patterns, his glowing speckles and bars and flecks of blue-bordered red-orange and carmine coming clear in what I hope will be the stream's healing bath. This beautiful but alarming freeze-frame ends in an instant as the fish rights himself in the amber water. His white-edged fins drift slowly forward; then with a surge he disappears among shadows and boulder-shapes, and scatterings of reflected landscape that undulate with his final tail-swirl.

Wading the Floodplain: 18 August

Even before I emerge from morning shadows in dense brush at the foot of the wooded slope that descends to the river, a great blue heron lifts up from the water's edge and wings off through the openings among the huge, wide-branching silver maples of the floodplain. At almost the same moment, a kingfisher flies downriver, with a short pause on an overhanging maple branch. The fish who live here would do well to keep an eye on the sky. Two painted turtles bask on a fallen log in a backwater lined with pickerel-weed where it borders the river and surrounded

Blacknosed dace (Rhinicthys atratulus)

by burreed and amphibious smartweed on its upland margins. The turtles tilt their gleaming shells to take the day's first sun.

With that same morning sun on my back, I walk upriver. The entire floodplain is a world of water at thaw and spring flood, and becomes one again after autumn rains and early snow; but in mid- and late summer, at the time of low water, the river drops away and keeps to its bed, leaving shelves of lush green growth on broad level plains with their islands of great trees. I follow a narrow deer trail through an expanse of sensitive fern, which along other brooks and streams is perhaps knee-high, but here reaches above my shoulders. It is impossible to see the wet ground beneath these sunlit green canopies, except where animals keep

pathways worn. I have to look up to admire a blue vervain, with its cobalt blue and violet flowers glowing intensely on tall spikes held several feet above the ferns. I could almost be in Lilliput: the rampant growth of the floodplain is not only dense, but also oversize, with familiar plants all considerably taller than anywhere else I encounter them. I turn away from the deer trail and feel my way through the growth, then descend to the river, where I begin a wade of muddy shallows. This amber sea, with its spreads of emergent plants, is far too warm for trout at 77°F, but in deep, riverine runs, in morning shadows and under banks, in riffles and dark pools under the trunks and tangles of fallen ancient trees, the water is at least 15° cooler. In such places, brown and rainbow trout hide. I would think the river's brook trout have moved upstream by now, to steeper gradients with mossy rocked runs and plunge-pools under white pine and hemlock, though there are shaded pools and gentle riffles, and refreshing mouths of spring-fed tributaries that could shelter them even in the floodplain. I keep this yearly appointment with the river's lower reach, to wade it at low water, and try for fish.

I see that another wader intent upon fish has passed here earlier in the morning. A line of heron tracks skirts the water's edge, perhaps set down by the same blue-gray bird who left the river to me a short time back. There are suckers and shiners aplenty in the warm, weed-choked river margins. I cross a sandbar, through willow outcrop-pings, wading over a barred sweep of white sand where gentle waves of windier days have created lasting traces of themselves on the river bottom. These sand-riffles are the tracks of the wind. The sun has just now reached a long, white-water riffle that races over bars and spreads of gravel after slicing through a beaver dam. I hide in willows and cast to the sparkling riffles, the only place along this languid run the river makes a sound. Before the fly drifts to the head of the pool it is taken from the surface with a shimmering flash. The morning comes alive in a silver fish in silver water. He runs, I turn him, a gleam in the river's clear streaming. The fish counters with a turn of his own, becomes a dark shape for a moment, then is lost in the rippling of the water. Unnerved at the thought of losing the possible trout (what is that electricity they send back through leader and line, time after time, year after year?), I am also put on edge by the apprehension that I have hooked a large fallfish, a silver chub. But now he leaps into the morning sun, and I see that the silver side is streaked with rose. Dark-spotted and shimmering, he leaps again. It is a thrashing rainbow trout I work into the shallows and finally up onto the sandbar, in shattered patterns of sunlight and tree shadow.

For the next half hour I fish the retreating shadows of the pool, taking one more rainbow trout, and catching and tossing back a number of fallfish. In morning shade the sandbar and its willow thickets are so agreeable, and playing the mirror-bright fallfish and occasional shiners in the clear water is such a pleasure that I am in no hurry to wade on up the river. At length I set out along the shallows, up toward the beaver dam. It is an extensive one, thirty-five or forty yards wide, and curiously open in the middle, where there is a five- or six-foot sluiceway through which water surges, creating the fish-pleasing conditions in the riffles and pool below. The situation is puzzling, as such an opening would seem to be caused by humans, yet the usual unmistakable evidence of such a demolition is nowhere to be seen. Nor does this appear to be an abandoned dam that has finally yielded to the river's insistence, for all along its unbroken lengths there are fresh-cut twigs, some still bearing leaves, indicating that beavers are keeping up with their structure. Perhaps it is a work in progress, or a restoration project. The dam seems ancient enough. Even with its central spillway, the dam appears to maintain a stable and suitable environment for beavers, and that may be the crux of the matter, though I am not familiar with such a deliberate flow-through-style beaver dam.

I cast above the dam, and a heavy and assertive fish takes my offering, just in the shadow of one of the silver maples. I come up over the beaver dam and play him out into the open shallows, much against his will, soon perceiving that I have hooked a large creek chubsucker. Carplike, large-scaled, bronze and amber-brown, he flares strong, red-tinged pectoral fins and turns against my pulling. I am captivated by his form and luster as he swims above his perfect fish-shadow in a shallow, transparent sea, against a green and gold background of sand, scattered water plants, and ropes of algae. Here is what appears to be a primeval, elemental fish, as tangible a member of his kind as I come upon. He swims for a time at my feet, deliberate

Creek chubsucker
(*Erimyzon oblongus*)

and outwardly unperturbed by his invisible tether. I wish him neither inconvenience nor terror, but there is a great pleasure in watching a fish swim in his river; the supple, copper-bright twists and turns, the rhythmic curlings and cuppings of a tail fin taking a hold in water, the erect, rippling dorsal fin counterpoised by stiffly set pectoral fins. His golden eye with its coal black center looks into the sky above the water. There can be no comfort for him in the larger-than-life heron towering above him, or in the mysterious impossibility of his turning back to deep water, shadows, and sunken trees. I get my hands around him as he thrashes at the surface, and appreciate his girth (which my hands cannot completely encircle) and the strength moving along the entire length of him. This is no ice-water and shadow trout, no fine-skinned, quicksilver life I am afraid to touch, but a fish-animal, plated with bronze and copper coin, who bears the holding and feels good in the hands. He seems like a fish from the seas of forever, and I feel for a moment like a forever-fisherman, holding water that has taken on life and become dream and substance, emblem and sustenance. A more deeply primal sense of going-after-fish comes to me, and as I look at this fish, so still for a moment in my clasping hands, I think back to a painting I saw years ago in Florence, a Renaissance painting of a youth and an old man, striding along a hill against a sky with surreal, linear clouds. As I remember, the youth looked up into the face of the old man; in any case, he carried a large and marvelous fish, silver-scaled and brushed with bronze, quite similar to the fish in my hands. The fish in the painting was lovingly entwined in an elaborate, well-ordered lacing and weaving of twine or leather, so well designed to the contours of the fish as to seem a part of its natural form. That image of returning with a fish at day's end intimates origins farther back in time and more seminal than the planting of the first corn. A sudden surge of strength ripples against my hands, and I am brought back to the river and its sun-bronzed fish, which I lower at once into the water. I gradually uncurl my fingers and withdraw my hands. An instant poised in midwater, and then a race that seems as swift as any trout's, and the dream and the reality of this river-dweller are lost in the shaded depths of the channel.

I move upriver. It becomes too deep to wade, so I thread my way through the endless fern-forest, keeping to deer trails. These end at times in well-trampled openings under spreading silver maples, where the deer have apparently bedded down for the night. I cut back to the riverbank every thirty to fifty yards and fish deep, dark holes among the fallen trees. I see fish here, but they keep their identities hidden, dark shapes for a moment only, tails disappearing, forms dissolving in watery shadows. I catch none of these living shadows.

I keep moving upriver, to where I can wade over gravel bars and sand mounds, among alternating riffles and log-strewn pools. I see two trout, parallel, tails waving in unison, beautifully spaced just beneath a long, shallow, tumbling riffle dropping abruptly into a wide pool. I am surprised to find them so much in the open on an August afternoon. They do not remain so for long: I approach from behind them, press my luck in drawing too close, and send them instantly into cover with my first cast. I am sure they have rehearsed this air-raid drill many times. There is no way to be certain now, but I have a feeling they were brook trout, and I have to believe it would be pointless to try to wait them out, or tempt them from cover with any kind of hooked enticement. I regret not having been more furtive, not having watched them longer. I am not likely to get back here any time soon.

I advance to the next arrangement of riffles and pools, to where tip-up mounds and sprawling trunks of yet-living red maples protect a pool that features skimming branches, heavy shade, upwelling currents, and surface drift. I feel I am close to trout here. There are two strikes in quick

Brown trout

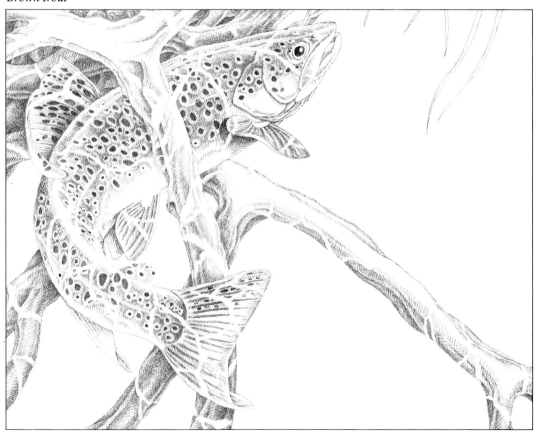

succession just off a branch overhang, but I fail to connect. I try beneath the surface, and on a long run of line well in under a bank of red maple and overhanging royal ferns, I am onto a fish. I set the hook against a hefty pull and work an energetic fish, who breaks up the filmy haze over a still section of the pool with rips of white water. When I get my first glimpse of the head of this strong and determined one, I could almost think I had hooked a burly pickerel in a rather unlikely setting, but even from some distance, black spots stand out on an olive-brown shape. It is a brown trout, one of the river's surprises.

When I make my occasional angling forays along this waterway, I fish rather generically, as though for cosmic trout. It is not quite so unpredictable as dropping a line into the ocean, but the range of takers along the river's varied reaches can be mystifying. When I catch a rainbow or brown trout in this river, I tend to have something of a "What are you doing here?" reaction. The former species, native to western mountains, and the latter, from far Germany, have come by circuitous routes to the waters of northeastern North America. In most cases, these and other introductions have not gone well for the indigenous species. Native brook trout have been displaced from many former strongholds as a result of the stocking of non-native fish. In this river, I do not believe that many, if any, of the brook trout are any more native to the drainage than are the brown or rainbow trout. They are hatchery-raised fish. The original intent of stock-ing trout was to provide urban anglers an opportunity to catch fish that would not possibly be available otherwise. As cities have multiplied and spread, with no end in sight, and have become linked together or been united by a proliferation of surburban areas, nearly all trout-fishing has come to be supported by stocking. Descendants of the original brook trout who filled this extensive, formerly quite favorable habitat live on now in remote tributary headwaters or the inaccessible reaches of inflowing brooks. This is a familiar scenario for native salmoid species in regions where they have not been extirpated altogether.

Since the mid-eighteen-hundreds, salmonids have been transplanted and mingled all over the world by humans who had little or no knowledge of what the biological or ecological consequences of their actions might be. Probably no vertebrate has been shifted around by human hands more than have the fishes. In the United States, more than 140 species of freshwater fish have become established in waters outside their natural range. Forty of these are not native to North America. Attempts have been made to establish many more species than these, but there have been failures. The mixing of species, and even of different stocks of the same species, combined with extensive degradation and alteration of waterways, has had a devastating impact on many salmonids in their native habitats. For many, anglers and non-anglers alike, it has not seemed to have mattered. Fish are fish, and recreation is recreation. Fortunately, fisheries have recently begun basing their practices on a better foundation in biology. However, hatchery-rearing, introducing non-native species, and the mixing of species and stocks of the same species that have not evolved in association with each other or with the ecology of the drainage systems into which they are introduced, continue to be practiced on a large scale, with no clear picture of the long-term effects.

Fish do not have to be transported across oceans to cause ecological perturbations; losses can result from simply spreading a species from one mountain range to the next, as has been the case with the rainbow trout. Native only to the Pacific slope, rainbows introduced into mountain streams harboring westslope and Yellowstone cutthroat trout have hybridized with these species to such an extent that few wild, pure genetic stocks of them now exist. Through human intervention, rainbow trout have been given more than a new mountain or two; they have been stocked worldwide, in every continent except Antarctica. Interbreeding among transplanted and native salmonids has been responsible for the loss of varieties of char that had been isolated in deep, cold, glacial lakes for millennia.

In addition to problems stemming from hybridization, many stockings, such as the introduction of brown and rainbow trout, have led to the displacement of native species. It might appear that two trout species with behavioral differences could share a stream or a river without negative predation or competition. Brook trout, for example, appear to prefer positions in slower currents adjacent to, or directly beneath, cover, while rainbow trout tend to frequent swifter-flowing water in riffles and runs out away from cover. There is no apparent significant predation by any life stage of one of these species on that of the other, and it would seem that these trout could cohabit a productive stream environment and share its resources. But over time—periods from ten to fifteen years—introduced rainbow trout displace native brook trout. Similarly, brown trout replace brook trout, even though the two species generally favor dissimilar habitat niches and water temperatures. In order to allow a truly noncompetitive separating out and cohabitation of a stream, the natural history of the two species would have to be extremely divergent.

As for fishery concerns, biological, ecological, and preservational awarenesses have begun to acknowledge and address a natural ethic and esthetic. The increasing emphasis placed by management on the value of wild trout in undisturbed ecosystems and of natural reproduction within native populations is an encouraging shift. It is to be hoped that one of the most lamentable downsides of stocking—the fact that it has been promoted, expanded, and heavily financed at the expense of protecting and restoring natural habitat—is beginning to be corrected. The fact that the phrase "...and their habitat..." so often follows the word "trout" in current management and sportsfishing discussions portends a desirable shift in agenda and dialogue. Efforts such as those to preserve heritage strains of brook trout in remote streams of the Adirondacks, which have miraculously been spared the introduction of non-native salmonids and genetically altered hatchery-raised fish of their own species, hint at a better day for wild trout, at least for some remnant populations. Hanging on in such restricted holdouts seems to be the fate of a majority of wildlife not already irretrievably lost. Over the past century, 27 species and 13 subspecies of North American fish have been declared extinct; and at present the American Fishery Society considers another 364 species and subspecies as endangered, threatened, or of special concern.

Spring-Fed Pool: 18 August

At day's end I make an excursion to the spring-fed pool in the headwaters of the river. I come to a familiar opening in the wooded borders of this reach and shoulder through meadow rue that reaches over my head, emerging into the blinding glare and heat still emanating from the late-day sun. A riffle over black stones above the great pool is one of the few water sounds I have heard in my wading today. Summer heat and drought have taken away, one by one, the many voices of the brooks and rivers.

Finding handholds among the alders, I ascend the precipitous bank at the tail of the pool, then walk along the ridge above the water. The trout are here. I see them here every year at low water, usually in mid-August. They line up in a narrow streaming of cold, clear water.

This spring runs briskly, unceasingly, only a short distance from where it bubbles out of the earth; it is as cool when it enters the river as it is when it leaves the ground. Such water keeps a rather constant temperature all through the year—between 45°F and 50°F, dramatically cooler than the high 60°F to low 70°F readings building up throughout many stretches of the river. The same seeps, springs, and spring-fed tributaries that enter and warm trout waters in winter, when the main flow is barely above freezing, are critical sources of cooling in summer. The course of this inflow is easy to trace, as it washes away all silt from its sluiceway and sweeps the white sand clean where it runs over the bottom of this tea-colored pool. Just downstream, where the inflow becomes diffused in the warmer waters, trout hover, their noses pointed into the chilled, oxygen-rich spring stream. At times they advance closer to its source, and are silhouetted against the white sand, a risk that indicates their need for relief from summer stress. I can count the ones who shift over the sand, or at least approximate a number. This is one of those times during which trout will tolerate close company. These are most likely stocked trout, inured to living fin-to-fin. It seems there are five above the sand shelf now, though even in such a fish-in-a-barrel situation, trout seem to appear and disappear without moving, and are difficult for my eyes to get a hold on.

I descend to water's edge and take a footing on a narrow ledge that is well beneath the surface in flood time. More as an experiment than a serious effort to hook a trout, I first fish the head of the pool, at the tail of the riffles. Predictably, I catch a fallfish, large and lively, and then a yellow perch. These warm-water fish are in their glory, and feeding in a frenzy. Possibly at dawn, after an all-night cooling, trout assert their place among them; but trout tend to be off their feed under these conditions, and may not even forage at the foot of the riffles or in shady undercuts along the banks. I wonder if there are any native trout left in this river and, if there are, if they come to this spring-fed pool, or whether they seek a

far more secretive seep or spring in remoter sections. I am sure that historically this was a major refuge for native brook trout.

I try the run of spring water, riding it with dry flies and wet, to the very noses of the trout, but induce no rise or stir. When I fall short, and present directly above them, they all scatter and fall back a bit, out of sight in the depths. But the lure of the ice-water is compelling, and within minutes they edge back up the shelf and face into the inrush once again. It is almost impossible to see them now, from my vantage point low to the surface, but they appear to hold true to trout hierarchy, with the largest at the forefront, by a nose. There are times when cold water is more critical than food to these

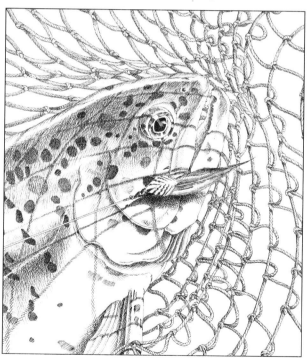

salmonids. Despite the stress factor, I would assume that any native trout would have disappeared at my initial approach, at so much as the stepping of my sneakers on the high bank, and not reappeared. I have not been particularly secretive, and have waded two strides into the pool to facilitate the tricky roll-casting from the crowding edge of the embankment and its overhangs of alder and dogwood. Those who would catch trout are advised against entering the water when it is low and warm, which unfortunately is when the rivers are the most pleasurable to wade. If they were not so pressed to keep to the cooling inlet, even these stocked trout would have taken flight by now. As I work this clear jet of water in the pool one more time, I see the lead trout-shape descend, in apparent pursuit into the darker depths. Why, after all of these casts, I cannot say. I am ready, and set the hook. I force the matter in bringing the fish to me, not wanting to play him overmuch under these trout-stressing conditions.

As gently as possible, I bring him to the net I use on occasion in more open conditions. He is a sizable rainbow trout, a hatchery fish who nonetheless bears an impressive blush of rose-violet all along his sides. Stressed as he is by his environment, the fish is valiant, and keeps up a determined struggle. Well hooked, held by a taut line, encircled by a net, the trout surges ahead, thrusts on, his body rippling against unbreakable netting as though it were water about to yield him freedom, and sanctuary. There is nothing in this trout that will give in to what holds him back; a fight like this, if prolonged, could bring fatal exhaustion. Low sunlight and long shadows cross the pool as I dislodge the hook and work the net away. The trout glides off, carrying his rainbow back into the pool. The glistening spring flows on and on, and will revive him.

Grape-Arbor Island: 24 August

I pause in amber stillwaters above the beaver dam, where the purposeful stalking of a great blue heron is revealed in a line of straight-toed tracks across the shallows. The steps have left a perfect pattern imprinted in the thin layer of mucky silt. It appears that the great bird was here not long ago. Looking behind me I observe the tracks my wading sneakers leave, not nearly so artfully or symmetrically aligned. The mingled record of the heron's and my passing this place intrigues me. These are not impressions of fossil duration, but for a time, perhaps even until the autumn rains set the brook to rearranging things again, two waders in the stream will have left an intermingled mark, a signature of sorts, in a fluviatile landscape.

Much work has been accomplished by water, muck, and sand. I see a crayfish beside a stone. His probing, ten-footed shufflings have made no mark, at least none that I can see. This savory crustacean has somehow avoided the mink who left a pile of rosy crayfish castings on a stone at the end of the beaver dam. He has dodged heron, turtles, trout, and a host of other predators to have attained such a size in this intensely hunted brook. The water level is down considerably, and the exposed mud flats of the brook's flood margin are well ornamented with the tracks of deer and raccoons. There is a constant sound of running water from a hidden trickle that eventually drops from the level of the beavers' pond and tumbles to the channel below. This channel, so fine for fishing when cool waters rushed through it, nearly until summer solstice, is now more suited to shiners and dace than trout.

I wade out of the brook and take to the shaded thickets, making an arc along the face of the ironwood slope and descending to the water near midpoint of the deep pool at the bottom of the steep rise. I have found brook trout here even on such dog days of summer as this. A sweaty struggle is required to get through the innumerable stems and branches of an ironwood hedge, and the downhill effort seems as strenuous as it is in going up. Once again at water level, I press my way through masses of royal fern so intergrown that traversing them seems another form of wading, and I am unable to avoid leaving a wake behind me. I cross a log to a small root island created years ago by the toppling of several large maples and am finally within casting reach of the pool. I don't know just how deep it is. I sometimes think of taking a sounding, but as yet it is one of this brook's unprobed mysteries. Something in its riverine darkness suggests to me that this pool is unfathomable, that no measuring of feet or yards would reveal its true depth.

Once on this little island, which is perhaps six feet wide by ten feet long, I move on all fours, as surreptitiously as I can. More wood turtle than mink, I achieve whatever stealth I can by means of slow movement. There is no standing up in this tangle. I am kept to the proper height for the minute delight of being here. If I can keep from causing the less-than-solid earth to tremble, I can go unnoticed in the shadows of the lacy leaf arbor that crowns this well-placed island.

From sheltering darkness at water's edge, I look out into the blinding August

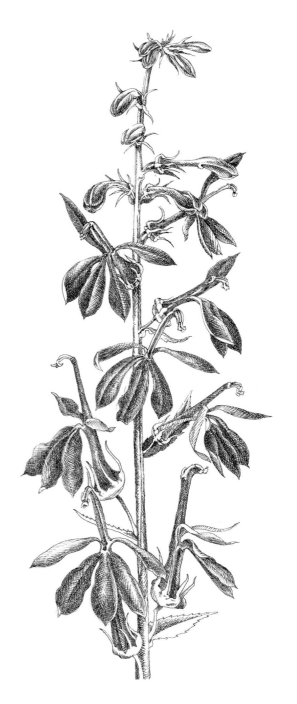

Cardinal flower (<u>Lobelia cardinalis</u>)

glare. The brilliance of cardinal flowers pierces the afternoon haze, their intense red literally leaping out from the surrounding landscape, their reflections streaking the water like slashes of fluorescent paint. The dark and brandywine pools of Blackwater Brook seem to be distilled more deeply here. Black-winged damselflies flit among the overreaching ferns. All else is completely still. The late afternoon holds its breath. It is too hot for birds to sing. I take my seat on a loosely woven mat of chewed beaver twigs, arranged and left lying on the wet mud by the lowering water. I extend my rod just beyond the outermost leaves of overhanging wild grape, and flip a line into the pool. In rather quick succession I take three small fallfish, shining silver minnows who brighten the water and enliven the sultry afternoon hour. It is not promising to fish the same spot after taking a minnow, let alone after catching three in a row; it would be reasonable to assume any brook trout of any size in the vicinity would have asserted himself by now, and sent the little silver ones packing. But this is not always the case, especially in a pool like this. There are deep, dark holdings, from which the trout will not advance beyond a line carefully drawn in water, no matter how tempting the offer. At dawn or dusk there may be a less restrictive set of limits. But the beauty of the place and the mood of the hour once again compel me, or is it lull me, into making stream-fishing a sit-and-wait affair, a rather unorthodox approach more suited to night-fishing for hornpout. A friend once told me,

as we fished a slow wide stretch of a small river that slid through a pine forest, to let my line lie still on the bottom, wait awhile, and then retrieve, employing a different retrieve each time. When I look for a reason not to move, I can take this strategy too much to heart. Shifting slightly on my mat of beaver branches, I reach out through a wreath of grapevines, and cast down the pool a bit, where something of a submarine logjam is suggested by a log-and-branch tangle extending above the surface. I wait, then work a twitching retrieve, up from the depths. A great surge at the surface brings me to my knees as I thrust my arms out from the grapevines, in an attempt to set a hook that is already gone. The empty line comes back, the leader (I recall that it was the most expensive leader) sheared off just above the hook. Snapped off might be a more accurate rendering, but something in the upheaval on the pool's surface, which has not been so much as dimpled the whole time I have been on the island, leads me to think it was sheared. Trout move in this dark water, I am certain.

The surface settles out before I do. My hands tremble as I set rod and line to rights, and prepare to test the logjam again. Neither skill nor composure is required this time, as I am onto a fish at once, in the same region as the recent attack. I bring a brook trout to the island, a vibrant, eleven-inch native slashing through the water on a steamy August afternoon. The fish in the Pool at Ironwood Slope are responding to something other than my fishing technique,

I have a feeling. A second trout hits the moment I am back in the water, but slips the hook. I am fishing at my fingertips now, and have a clear view of the returning streamer as it flashes near the surface in a slant of hazy sunlight filtering through the grape leaves to my head and shoulders. At the same moment, in the same light, I see another flash, the trout's splendid rush to retake his quarry. All the langour of the preceding afternoon hours is dispelled by this thrilling moment, though the landscape itself does not change its face. There is time within a second to allow a perception of the coal black eye and its glint of gold, a gold of substance, light, and life. And I see the patterns and colors along the surging back and sides of this wild fish, down to the lavender-haloed crimson spots along his lateral line. I try to hold onto these instants within hours and days. They possess a time outside of time.

Given a second chance, I do not lose the trout again. I slide him onto a silky dogwood stringer, alongside the first, who is longer by a nose than the new one. I had brought this slender branch of forking twigs with me to the island. A tradition since my earliest days of fishing for trout has been to cut a maroon-red, opposite-branched twig of silky dogwood for carrying any fish I might catch, this ubiquitous shrub of wild streams having taken on the status of a totem in this regard, or at least as a symbol of good luck. The two trout feel hefty on the

Brook trout on silky dogwood stringer

branch. Suspended in air, there is so much beauty left in them, although the life has been taken from them, so much fluid grace remaining, even in their stillness. It strikes me that there is a nobility in them yet; their open eyes are neither horrifying nor depressing, and even the implicitly brutal image of them hanging by their gills from a stick is more fascinating than unsettling. I think of the many drawings and paintings of

fish, still-life works with fish on platters, on stringers, strewn along the banks of rivers and streams, the shores of lakes and oceans. Always they are a compelling image, and among the seemingly endless array of fish forms and patterns, colors and designs, the salmonids appear to me to reign supreme. And yet there is the realization that these eyes, which find a glint of daylight even in deepest shade, will never again see the wine red depths of this pool, the flickering threads of golden sunlight in the channel above it, the silver cascades of floodwater plunging over the beaver dam. And there is the awareness, equally inescapable and more sad than death, that vast numbers of these wild fish and their wild places have been taken outright or altered out of existence by human actions, and that the menaced sanctuaries such as this one I sometimes fish are being encroached upon by the hour. We establish limits for the taking of fish, but put no limits on the taking of wild lands and waters; we can stock fish, but we cannot put back wildness. One must be so careful in the taking.

I turn back to the pool, which has long since closed back over in silence and utter stillness. Preparing to fish, I watch the water and see a white cabbage butterfly appear suddenly, its struggling wings trapped on the surface. This is an odd place for a butterfly of open fields. I certainly have noticed no breeze or any disturbance to account for this entrapment. There will be no escape. The surface film has taken a hold more tenacious than that of any spider web,

and those fluttering white wings were meant for the driest air. Even in the absence of wind or rain, the stream collects living things from the land, and these unfortunate terrestrials become prey for trout. The drift here is imperceptible to me; but I see that this bright white form has been carried slightly downstream from the point at which I first noticed it. The butterfly's valiant efforts vibrate a series of rapidly widening rings over the surface as his wings try to lift him, but there is no flying in this reflected sky. I no sooner wonder about trout than trout appears. A sudden dark swirl and rush, then a shallow whirlpool in which the bedraggled butterfly continues to struggle. Something immediately detectable in the taste or texture of this terrestrial will keep it from becoming trout food. On the basis of this field trial under the most natural conditions, I decide that I will never recommend that anyone attempt to tie a white cabbage butterfly imitation, however intriguing and artistic the resulting fly might be.

I return to my fishing, catching a small yellow perch. Some warm-water invaders maintain a presence in this realm of the trout. But the latter apparently have the advantage here, as the environment does not allow the establishment of significant populations of species that would compete with the native trout for food and space. In streams like this, but where conditions have been altered to favor the warm-water species, native trout retreat, decline, and often die away. The trout-favoring qualities of this brook are underscored as I land an eight-and-one-half-inch native. It could be that in the disturbance of my catching the perch and tossing him back, larger trout withdrew into hiding places, and this younger one took his turn in the temporarily uncontested feeding lane. Or it could be that he is now the largest in this niche, after my hooking of the previous two.

With curiosity now my primary motivation, I flip my line out one more time. I also have in mind that this will be my final cast...unless I cast one more time. The final cast of any fishing sojourn is one on which all who fish bestow great consideration, if not outright meditation. It is often a firm decision subject to reconsideration, whether it reels in a fish or an empty line. On this occasion, I meet with a fish. As I turn him I see the black-barred, green-bronze side of a small perch. All fins erect and flared, he twists and pulls, shuddering head-down in combative resistance to the restraining line. His white belly glows as he revolves out of the sun-slant, straining for darker, deeper water. I reverse the fish, and draw him toward the surface. He struggles all the more. Just as I shoulder out through the grapevines to deal with the perch situation, I see a great, dark shape in the water, a shadowy, high-speed, onrushing fish. All in one moment my heart leaps at the recognition of the kind of fish that has launched this assault, I realize that I have revealed myself to the charging trout, and I see the sudden, powerful reversal of the attacker, with an instantaneously disappearing show of reddish bronze and white. There is a

"schloop" in the water as the force of the submarine turning sends a black swirl of heaving water outward across the pool. A dark sink forms deep in the water behind the upheaval of the first wave. This spreading surge washes against the far bank, and I am shaken as I watch the progress of the widening rings. Then a memory of a time from the earliest point in the year comes to me, and I remember standing in the snow not far from here and feeling a monstrous pulling of my line deep beneath the ice. Now deep in hiding, there is somewhere in this stream a brook trout who would think nothing of taking on an injured perch over five inches long. A fish to inspire dreams, and intensify the thoughts of return that accompany every departure from the stream.

Fishing Until Dark: 29 August

In the evening, water sings softly over the lip of the beaver bowl below a knoll of aspen and sweetfern. A three-day deluge, heavy rain circling in on the violent winds from a hurricane's having passed off the distant coast, has recharged every waterway on short and sudden notice. The trout will not have to await the more gradual refilling of autumn rains this year; a flood almost equal to that of the thaw has changed their world nearly overnight. Day's last light has recently slipped away from the highest crowns of trees far across the wet meadow. Its final traces fade on the few clouds lingering just

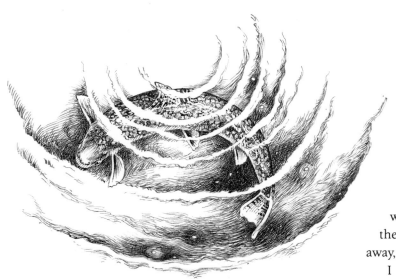

slow journey some-where, go purple-gray, taking a touch of silver from the moon. My only fish connection so far has been with medi-um-sized pickerel taken on a green-gold strike close by the weedy bank. He shook off the hook and was quickly away, happily for both of us.

I cast just short of the upreaching fingertips of silky willow across the pool. The rising water and the weight of its ripening berries have brought the brook and silky dogwood together, and its fruits lie in the current's caress. I work alder borders and dogwood sweeps, the nightlike darks beneath the ferns and sedges. As I retrieve, there is a sudden tak-ing, at my feet, just as I was about to lift my line out of the water. One is so easily lulled along a stream, and the alertness that should accompany even the last inches of a line's play in the water is hard to maintain. I set the hook too sharply, and am in the alder branches at my shoulder. Even in this dusky water I saw enough to identify a brook trout. They are settling themselves back out throughout the brook; the wild trout have returned with the rains to reclaim their springtime haunts.

I leave the moonrise and the bur-bling water at the dam and make my way into inky thickets where nightfall has

above the eastern horizon, with peach blushes surrendering to violet. The moon, within a day of its full face and as startled-looking as ever, now advances up and out from behind a dark, solitary pine.

I descend to alder thickets at land's end, to watch and wait. The dark shadow I have been anticipating darts in the water, and against a moon-pale section of the pool's bottom I see the nearly square tail and the white-edged fins. A small trout moves at twilight. In the oncoming darkness, black animal shapes appear; furtive, small, sudden mammals emerge from grass and ferns and race about the opposite banks. Mice, moles, or voles...I cannot tell what they are as they run with quick splashings in and out from cover. One literally runs across the water, leaving a rippling, silver trail in lieu of foot-prints. The moon brightens and becomes burnished gold as the sky goes rose-violet all around it. Thin clouds, on their long, already taken over, along the quickening run below the dam. Trout can see better than I. Their gold-ringed eyes are adapted to seek food on either edge of daylight, so that they are able to detect the tiny motes they pursue in the earliest radiating of predawn light or on the star-brightening verge of night, when it seems that water holds the last of the day's light longer than the air does. It is at these times that many stream and river insects make their moves, and trout are attuned to them, capable of tracing their shadowy darts toward the surface, or their flickering movements upon it. Only night itself can close the lidless eyes of trout, who hover in the darkest undercuts, in unlit hollows among great stones, or the blackness of sunken logs and trailing fountain moss. The darkest night has its even darker shadows, and here trout sleep, open-eyed, suspended in drifts of water, shifting at times to hunt by starlight.

I come up out of the brook and begin my ascent of the knoll. Earth seems less tangible than water now. The landscape itself blurs and dissolves with nightfall's advance, yet its features are sharply defined in reflections on the water. A single whip-poorwill call, a solstice echo somewhat out of place so late in the season, sounds above the faint murmur of the brook. Not long after, the first star appears in the eastern sky. I make a wish, bid the trout good-night, and leave the darkening brook to continue flooding the shadow-landscape through which it flows.

Turning Leaves and Early Dark

Time is but the stream I go a-fishing in.

—*Henry David Thoreau*

Midges: 3 September

Strong, late-day winds are blowing upstream, against the steady drift of the current. Minute insects, visible only in the sun, weave a darting dance at a precise, unchanging level just above the water. Occasionally two meet in a dizzying circle, each spiraling around the other like skaters in the air. I have not seen a fish leap once at the scores of these whirling dervishes. Nor is that surprising, as not a single one would appear to offer a decipherable target.

The wind dies down across the water. I cast into a mirror gone blue-silver, and guide my shiny spoon along the brook's darkening edges, where, as the mild autumn

evening settles in, big fish are once again in pursuit of little fish.

Rainbow in the Rain: 4 September

A light rain comes up, a silent approach of tiny, widely spaced raindrops. I would not be able to detect this shower from my hiding place, which is roofed by white ash and red maple trees, if I did not see the scattering of little rings appearing and disappearing all across the pool. I work a deep run of broken water below a beaver dam, extending my rod surreptitiously along a beaver-felled tree, and casting up and over a stand of silky dogwood, across open water, to a precise point upstream of a boulder. I would not be likely to repeat such a deftness in presentation, to a more promising lie. But for all my intent and art, I find no takers. There is always the anticipation that such skillful and well-targeted casts will meet with immediate success, no matter how long a history one may have of their falling on empty waters, or failing to raise a visible trout. We tend to feel the perfect presentation has the power to create the result.

I ascend the bank and circle to the dam itself, crawling down to the point at which it joins the shore at the base of a red maple and a massive, long-dead elm. This dam is built tightly against the steep, boulder-strewn shore, and worked tightly around and among the trunks and buttressing roots of the trees, so integrated into the streambank that it seems to be an extension of the landscape itself. I slither over outcropping roots and underneath the cinnamon ferns, to a foothold on the beaver's solid construction, from which I can work the pond above. Dark amber water, reflecting bits of sky, is decorated with scatterings of the first autumn-tinged fallen leaves, and patterns of quickening rain. Here, a simple flip of line to the middle of an open beaver pool brings an immediate strike, and swift run of line. I can only think it is a fallfish, but the hook is set, and the fish-life at the end of my line triggers all the old instincts. The line is taut, then slack, as sharp pulls alternate with troubling emptiness. Suddenly the rain-spattered surface erupts with the water-shedding leap of a glimmering trout,

silver blushed with rose. In this unlikely place, I catch a rainbow in the rain.

Fishing Blind: 10 September

Having decided to fish from the eastern margins of the Pool at Ironwood Slope, I creep across the beaver dam and wade a race of silver streamlets through the dogwood shallows at its end. In my crossing I notice rocks, from the size of a child's fist to a grapefruit, resting underwater on the pond side of the dam. I am arrested by the placement of these stones on the sloping submarine wall of branches, leaves, sand, silt, and mud; they had to be placed there by the broad-tailed builders of this dam. I am not familiar with the beavers' use of stone in their remarkable constructions. Several particularly round ones have been set atop the dam, at the very edge of the detained water. The way in which they are arranged tempts me to think there is more ornament than function in their use. Perhaps, as with some walls built by human hands, they represent a combination of utility and incidental esthetics, as well as a practical solution to the matter of where to put the rocks that are a by-product of pond-building.

So often I want to stop and play with stones in a stream. Something about them compels attention, something about their water-brightened colors and patterns, the spaces between them, the shadows they

Rainbow trout

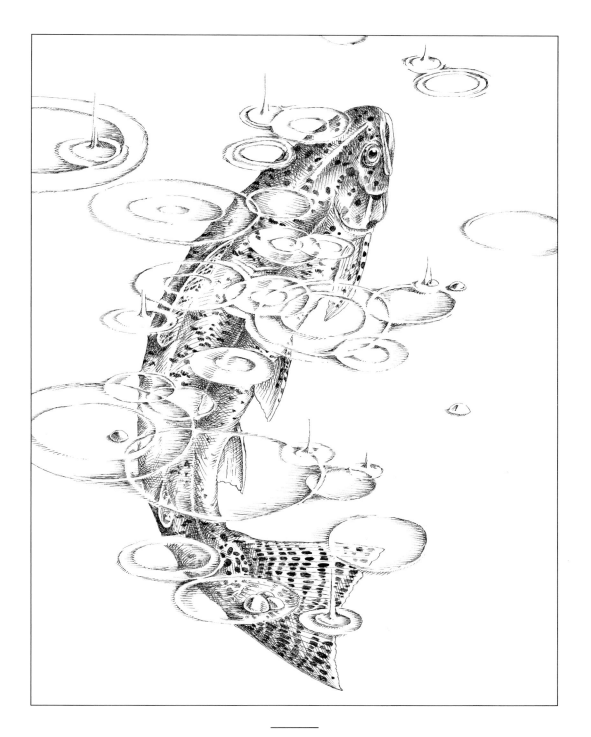

Spawning brook trout

cast. Arrangements of stone, in water or on land, whether set in place by shiftings of the earth, changings of the ocean's tides, the runnings of streams and rivers, or the conscious workings of ancient human hands, establish designs, create markings in the landscape that seem as if they should be decipherable. There is an eloquence in the silence and stillness of stones. Their intermingling with water and air is a dialogue that seems to speak of time.

Circling through the deep shade of white pines to arrive at midpool, I cast beneath a stand of silky dogwood. The air above the pool is completely still, though unruly winds agitate the upper pine branches. Mirrored in the water, these create waves of undulating green on the unmoving sur-face. There is open sky somewhere; a slit of blue lies on the stream. In the blue shape on the water I am startled to see reflections of leafless trees, and look up to confirm that the red maples in the edgewater shallows of the beaver pond have already lost all their leaves. Those further downstream, on slightly higher ground, begin their most intense flaming. It seems I often make my first discoveries about the state of the earth and sky in something I see on the water.

Sun-slants break across the crowns of the high pines just behind me, the pool stays dark in the shadow of the ironwood slope, as I present to the slight drift, attempting to slip a nymph into the depths along the log outcrops and their sunken branches. Fishing blind, as I nearly always do, I play the line with the tips of the fingers of my left hand. Sometimes I close my eyes. The feel of the intangible water and the workings of the all but weightless line come clearer to me then, my fingertips are better able to read the signals of the faintest electricity, the remotest pulse. I turn all senses inward, and can think that if I become attuned enough, I will feel the approach of a trout. My right hand, a separate intelligence, works the rod, with a broader sensibility. Years ago, a friend who was teaching me how to fish told me of a blind man in his town who was by far the best trout fisherman in the area, working all kinds of water under any conditions, often from a boat. It seemed incredible to me at the time (I had enough trouble with open eyes), but as I came into something of my own sensing and feeling of the unseen in the water, I could understand and believe. Sight is bewildering, and can confound. Along the densely thicketed

waterways I frequent, I often cannot distinguish between landscape and its reflection. Eyes closed, I am my fingertips and a nymphal insect in the deep pool.

Nearly everything a trout eats, 90 percent and up of his food, is an insect in one form or another, alive or recently dead upon the water. And as great a percentage of these nymphs, larvae, drifting terrestrials, and entrapped adult aquatics are poor swimmers, not truly creatures of open water. Generally, they are crawlers, wrigglers, or burrowers in the substrate and detritus of

the stream. When they are in the water column, away from cover, it is usually involuntarily, or for that brief and perilous journey to the surface film that separates their two worlds and their two lives, where they split the encasements of their watery life and escape on wings into an existence in the air.

A slight slipping of the line in my fingertips opens my eyes to the image of the ironwood slope in the pool. My left hand and my right wrist have done their work; the nymph with which I have been drifting is now a hook set in the jaw of a powerfully alive and resisting fish. Memories of transitory encounters with the exceptional pulling of a large trout come to mind at once. Shaking, I wade a step toward the careening pull against my forcefully bent rod, in an attempt to steer the trout from the logjam. There is not likely a mightier fish in this brook; he is wildly strong in the autumn water. I see him as a surge in the water, feel him as the wild heart of all this brook and its surrounding landscape. My own heart races, I want to throw my rod into the ferns and brush at the banking, and hand-over-hand the line, to bring the trout within my reach. There is an unrelenting jerking on the frighteningly bent rod, I let him run, then try to guide, admonishing myself to stay within myself, regain composure, and abandon force for finesse. As anxiety-ridden as I am, I somehow know I will see this fish, at least see him. But the mirroring surface of this overcast day is impenetrable, the pool beneath it unfathomable. There can be no sunlight over my shoulder to light my way into the water. I restrain the trout from diving hard, back down into holes beneath the log mazes, but there are tangles everywhere, this is no clean-swept, smooth-stoned mountain stream.

I take small steps sideward and slightly back, inching toward land, playing the bulldogging trout. White belly, bronze flash, he is nearer than I thought, then gone from sight. A brook trout absolutely, a brook trout who must be over sixteen inches. He veers along the shallow shelf extending from the eastern shore. Then the line holds taut, feels hard and unalive. All communication is lost. The vibrant life and staccato rhythms of the trout's valiant fighting are cut from me; and my own energies (how must these feel to the trout?) are severed from him. I see a flash of white, a great bronze turning in the water. The trout is still hooked. He has wound the line around underwater branches; our dialogue of opposing forces is broken off by the immutable interruption of waterlogged wood. On our own respective ends of the line, we each contend now with our own separate energies.

This situation is no good at all, neither for fish nor for fisherman, and is the one thing I truly wanted to avoid. The pool slopes away quickly at about the point where I saw the trout's last turning. Already waist-deep in the brook, I wade out to him, believing I may well end up swimming. Bending over at just the right angle, I can shift the dark reflection of a pine to where I think the trout is tethered, so that it breaks up the surface glare, and I can see into the

water. The big trout shudders up from the bottom, shaking his head from side to side, is halted abruptly by the line, bucks wildly against it, then settles back into concealing depths. He is brilliant, with a stippling of crimson and abundant spots of gold. He is green-black, green-gold, and bronze as he sinks out of sight with slow, serpentine waverings. I am nearly within reach of him, or at least of the leader I cannot see. My chin is to the water as I grope for the line, I am soaked to my armpits and wonder now why I did not at least leave my vest in the alders before setting out into this pool.

The fish rises again, twisting, his red-bronze flanks and white belly electric in the ambered darkness. The hook and line hold against his thrashing ascent. This trout could be a foot and a half long. My reachings put him in a frenzy, he slashes this way and that as he tries to break free from a line he cannot see and I cannot feel. I must at least cut the line. My face all but in the water, I hold completely still. The brook trout rises, slowly this time, I see him take form in the water, emerge from nothingness into being. This is no way to play a fish. He must be nearing exhaustion. His mouth gapes, his gills work strenuously, but there seems a calm in his sleek, streamlined body, which becomes the outward embodiment of poise and grace in the water. He turns, I can look him in the eye. Without taking my eyes from his, I move as slowly as I possibly can, to scissor my submersed arms through the water like someone feeling for a doorway in a pitch-black room. In all this watery space,

my fingers somehow find the thread that holds the fish. I stop all movement. Strangely, the big trout glides toward me, so that I can almost touch him. The line grows slightly taut as I begin to draw him to me. He arches sharply inward at midspine, flexes his head and tail stiffly upward, tail fully spread, mouth agape, and shudders violently all along his body, like a wild horse trying to break a rope, then turns sideways before me. I am moved by the brook-trout-patterned length of him. Trying to be imperceptible, I sweep my arm, drawing the line closer. There is no tension at all. I am stunned by the realization that it no longer holds this marvelous fish. He is so near me I could count his crimson spots. An instinct rushes through me, to lunge and grab the hovering trout. Does he know that all ties are broken between us, save the love I feel for all his wildness in his wild place? The brook trout is life and landscape. Theoretically, I could touch him; but there is no seizing this fish now, he might as well be a hundred yards downstream as within inches of my fingertips. He turns, and in a slow, descending glide, fades out of sight in the depths of his pool. For a moment, there is that sense of loss again, strangely piercing on this occasion, though there would have been no keeping this trout.

Fishing the Beaver Wake: 21 September

Below a beaver dam I approach a slow-drifting run that enters a deep, lowland

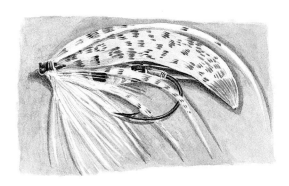

pool. Last year I caught September trout here on this same day, at this same late-afternoon hour. All is deeper now, the slow-moving depth that comes from a backing-up of the water. I brush my way through streamside cover and enter the water, wading the mucky bottom close to shore and using a line of winterberry holly as a breakwater for the ripples I cause. I get ready to cast over the cranberry-colored surface. The silky dogwood leaves have gone red, and in some places are as maroon as the autumn shadows. A beaver has been active all the while, cutting silver wakes in the water above his dam. Just as I prepare to let fly my line, the beaver, who has been aware of me since my arrival, comes to the brim of his pond, eyes full upon me, and slips up over the lip of the dam and on down over it, as fluidly as water.

The beaver swims the channel toward the pool, passing by me in a stately glide, unhurried, and for all outward appearances unconcerned. The water surges strongly with his passage and his wake obliterates the last vestiges of my rippling

entrance into the brook. No need now to worry about my presence being transmitted through this run: I will not be fishing quiet waters. As much as I would like to think myself welcome to my place in the stream, I know a protest will be lodged. An order has been established here: the beaver comes and goes at will, the dam serves as a chipmunk highway, warblers flit throughout the alders and dogwood, deer drink and browse at water's edge, glittery dragonflies wing above the pool, trout shadows swirl within it, and the sun crowns the tall pines above the brook; all of these in the season's own streaming are an established order. And I, for all my human awareness and sense of kinship here, inevitably come as an intruder, however much at home I may feel at times. His eyes taking me in all the while, the beaver arcs around a large outcropping of tussock sedge and royal fern, entering the pool below. This very outcropping at the narrow entrance to the pool is the intended target of my first cast. The gliding beaver silently turns to face me. And then comes the statement I expect, the resounding "ka-woosh" of the tail-slap, shattering the deep autumn quiet over the pool. Wondering what effect this explosive demonstration might have on the trout—it must feel like a depth-charge along their finely tuned lateral lines—I ready my line and cast. Emboldened, or maybe simply perturbed by my apparent lack of respect for or response to his warning smack, the beaver swims toward me. It appears he will want to see what sort of license permits me to wade and fish his watery dooryard. I am retrieving my first cast as he moves up to face me, meeting me eye-to-eye from a few yards off. He turns tail-end to me, arches his back, and fires a smashing shot at the surface, splaying water all about, bringing a rain of brookwater down upon my head and shoulders, and instantly setting off what appears to be a circular tsunami, a widening ring of dark, heaving water.

At this precise instant I see the unmistakable bronze flash of a brook trout's taking and turning. I set the hook, the line begins to run. I know by the strike that this is a good-sized native. Accustomed to his rudder-tailed neighbor's dramatic surgings and shock-wave expressions in the brook, and taking no apparent heed of these dynamic protestations or alarms, the trout has darted into the shallows on a pursuit of his own, and seized supposed food even as the water was scattered black and white all around him. It may be that the disturbance attracted the trout; I recall how quickly dace and other small minnows congregate over any area of the streambed I rile up in my wadings, searching my very footprints as I depart them, looking for any nymphs, larvae, or crustaceans stirred loose by my passing. Evidently what worries beavers does not trouble trout...a careless footfall on the bank would seem to cause them far more alarm than all this watery cannonading. I imagine they may even know the difference between an angler's falling in the drink and a beaver's warning slaps. We all have our own perils to face. I am sure a beaver would

not flick an ear at a kingfisher's winging over the pool, the very shadow of which would put trout down to stay, for quite some while. Having had his say, the beaver slides on down the stream as I set a splendid thirteen-inch native free beneath the dusky autumn landscape regathering on the quieting pool.

Kingfisher at Willow Pool: 1 October

As I come up to the crest of the high ridge above Willow Pool I hear a resounding splash. My first thought is that a beaver has let fly with a tail-slap, but almost at once I see a kingfisher alight on one of the dead willow branches overhanging the pool. She has caught a silver minnow and holds it crosswise in her scissored beak. With a series of short, sharp jerkings of her head and maneuverings of her bill she turns the fish, which is brilliant in the morning sun, so she can swallow it headfirst. Here is a real fisherman, and she certainly eats fresh fish. The swallowing, which is more of an engulfing, does not take long. But the ensuing perching and preening are quite unhurried. This bird's bath, breakfast, and morning meditations are impressively integrated. For all the time she spends on her wings, back, and tail, she does not groom her crest, which one might take for some center of her pride. It is still wet and scraggly-looking from her fishing plunge, and does little to reduce her head's oversized appearance. Perhaps the watery mirror below her is too distant to present a troubling self-image. I

Kingfisher (<u>Megaceryle alcyon</u>) with minnow

they had to be caught with a mouth or a foot. Something prompts this blue-winged fisher to fly off. She never noticed me in my screen of autumn-tinged black cherry leaves.

Trout and Cranberries: 4 October

I set out for a deep slow run of brook, reached by way of a cranberry-sedge meadow. I have been late this year in gathering cranberries from the mazes of vines lacing the turf here. Perhaps the sheltering sedges have insulated them against the first light burns of frost; in any case, their fruits are firm and their deepening red alerts me that I must pick some on my way out.

It will be a several-hundred-yard walk through this wet meadow along the ankle-deep deer and muskrat trails, and then a thigh-deep wade through a backwater creek before I reach the intended stretch of water. I lose a little time, a lot of energy, and a bit of my patience as I miss my signpost red maple tree due to the thinning of the leaves. The near and distant landscapes have been transformed by the season's progress, and what was well known to me in my springtime passing here has become confusing, and I am late in realizing that I have taken the wrong stand of white pines in the distance as my bearing, and that

marvel at such a fish-eater, thinking of the difficulty of netting a single minnow from a large school in a small pool. Not to mention the challenge of simply sighting a fish in the water. This the kingfisher does, and dives, and keeps focused on her prey in the blinding speed of her surface-shattering plunge from her world into that of the fish. And then, in the water she seizes and holds the slipperiest of prey with her mouth. I have seen osprey do the same with their feet. One would think that these darting minnows and high-speed trout would live forever if

at some obscured intersection I have shifted to the wrong animal path. I have been guided considerably out of my way and am forced to struggle through near-impenetrable "islands" of shrubby alder and red maple, each of which is ringed by a murderously thorned barrier of swamp rose, before I reorient myself to the inlet of the cranberry-sedge-meadow creek. I have not anticipated such an arduous physical involvement with the day's landscape, which is so benign in its October-mellowed appearance.

At length I reach the proper corner of the wet meadow, find the trickle that widens into a small creek and finally becomes a deep channel as it joins the main brook. The seep that initiates this creek, which becomes at once an inlet and a backwater of the brook proper, seems to come out of nowhere; its precise beginning cannot be pinpointed in the wet meadow turf and its sweeps of sedge, grass, and shrub. Muskrats like this creek. Here and there on its banks are flattened remains of muddy muskrat food-gathering and eating stations, strewn with their equivalent of ingredients for a bamboo-shoot soup.

Once I get to where I can recognize the red maple marking the meeting of the primary animal path and the creek, the whole landscape falls into place, and everything becomes familiar again. I know just where among the sedges and sweetgale I will come upon a colony of pitcher plants. This landscape within the landscape is on the intimate side by any real hiking standards, but twenty or so acres are enough to get me turned around, and for moose to roam on occasion; I have seen their tracks in the muck where the upland slope gives way to the wet meadow. I wade into the creek, where the going is much easier. Here I can take in the scenes surrounding me without having to find or fight my way among them. I walk and wade through autumn.

Dragonflies wheel in the open air, but the birds have gone. It is quieter now, without the red-winged blackbirds, though the song of the crickets never ceases. Grasshoppers leap as I brush the overhanging creekside growth; and although she is brilliant green in a world going to straw, a katydid disappears at once upon landing in a stand of bluejoint grass. When I get to the trout's part of this world, I'll have to try some terrestrials.

At the creek's joining the brook I come to one of my favored corners of this wetland. Nearly up to the limits of my waders I am engulfed in two worlds, immersed in water and surrounded by the rampant growth that reaches out over the brook above my head. The bottom drops away quickly here, to a pool too deep to wade. It lies over pure sand. I take hold of an outreach of sweetgale, gripping tightly enough to bruise some aromatic buds, and work my boots into a foothold on the precipitous mucky slope. I wait for the ripples of my last wading steps to settle out across this still section of the brook. As usual, I have moved very slowly. It would be risky to do otherwise because of the unpredictable depths and varied substrates along this route. The day itself seems to call for going slowly, and the trout, if they are here, require the same if I am not to scatter them to watery nether regions.

I work the shadowed overhangs along the opposite shore, skirting from one stand to another along the steep submarine slope, clinging to temporary ropes of twisted tussock sedge and sweetgale twigs. Thigh-deep in mud and water, I come as close to rock-climbing as I will ever come. I catch three brook trout in the time it takes the shadows of the alders to cross the brook, encompass me, and creep up over the dense growth behind me. How blue the shadows are among the grass, and how quickly they cool. I gather the trout from a spray of wild cranberry at brook's edge...this will be supper enough for two, providing they have eaten regularly of late. This is the day to try wild trout and wild cranberry.

I wade back out the creek, into agreeable sunlight once again. I feel as though I am wading back in time, to an earlier part of this same day. The sun is at my back as I knee my way through the growth lining the narrow animal trails. Cranberries spread before me, woven among the sedge and sweetgale. Vines are everywhere, lined with tiny, oval leaves, rich green, maroon, and deep red. The fruits are most abundant along the borders of the passageways, and where especially boggy pools forbid a roothold to other plants. Here the crimson berries are most striking against the wet, dark green of sphagnum moss. They are close to invisible in the shadows, and I pick

them more by feel than by sight. This proves painful in hollows where sharp-thorned swamp rose has twisted its way among the vines. But on the whole the gathering of these wild fruits is a pleasant accompaniment to fishing trout from the stream.

Last Day of Trout Season: 15 October

I will make my final casts of this year in the Pool at Ironwood Slope. My trout-fishing will end, but my trout season will not; I will wade until ice-in, then walk the ice while waiting for the thaw. Somehow, there is always time around me, though time is ever moving on, as water continually surrounds trout, while forever flowing on. The face of mid-October is reflected on the water, images held in place, the brook sliding by beneath them. The season itself seems a stream. Recent days have been still, and heavy-misted. With no winds to disturb the leaf-drop, trees can be recognized by the cloaks lying beneath them, the gowns they have dropped at their feet. Minnows school over a sunlit sandbar, turning sidewards in clear water for half-instants to flicker silver against gold. I hear the steady trickling of a tiny waterfall, and two notes from a hidden bird; the quieting of the year has already begun.

The drifting water brings me to the run and backwaters above the Pool at Ironwood Slope. The sun is low, the water is high, the beaver dam is now a waterfall with a riverine roar. There are myriad insects and

larvae in the deep new leaf litter in sidewater pools of the channel, just below the dam. Darting swiftly, like schools of miniature fish, they flee my entering feet. There is food in this clear stream, a fullness, it would seem; and though the water has been chilled, the cycles, however slowing-down, go on. After a succession of nights of hard frost, the brook is 45°F. Mid-October sunlight is amber in the stream. Large bubbles, fragile perfect domes of water, ride the race below the beaver dam. Long-lived for such insubstantial structures, they are carried for yards downstream before they suddenly are no more, though none reaches the great pool itself. For the length of their ride on the brisk water, each reflects on its south-facing arc a perfect, brilliant miniature sun, a near-blinding point of light.

I take my place and fish the pool, and it is not long before my line is lively with a trout. He feels brisk, as though energized with the brook's glittering reflections. I walk him to the shallows as he kicks water everywhere, then grab the line at the small hook's shank. For a moment the trout lies still, shimmering, sideways at the surface. This will be my last such look at a brook trout, and it will not last long. There is full autumn splendor in the color of this eleven-inch male. As colors die away along the stream, they seem to come alive in the trout. This male's colors are all on fire: blue aureoles smolder with purple around electric, crimson spots. All the yellows in him have gone gold, not lemon-gold, but an intense, radiant cadmium. His fins are strangely cold-looking, red-maroon flames, edged in jet black and a final slash of white as sharp as new snow. His belly glows, and is flushed with a red so deep it appears to go black. I twist the hook and he is gone in a brief curl of water.

I release this trout thinking that the fishing could go far too well here. To take the gold-ringed eyes and bronze flashes from this dark water would be to take the dark, sun-reflecting eyes of the streamside warblers, their bright-winged flittings among the alder shadows; or the gold fleckings of the wood turtle's shells, and the red-orange strokings of their legs in the same dark pools. Taking this trout would be like taking the slap of the beaver's tail, or the water's murmur over stones. There must always be trout. I break down my rod. I will walk the brook until the hills go blue, and shadows enclose the wetlands. The sun is gone so early now, and so quickly followed by night.

Young-of-the-Year: 18 October

Most branches are bare now. The brook is lined with umber leaves and folding ferns. Woodland grass is still erect but bleached, its sharp leaf-tips are white as frost. The season seems to have been brought to earth. The sun sweeps in a low arc, and even though they are leafless, thickets of alder and willow darken early. Lengthening nights with their successions of frost have slowly burned the color from the landscape,

113

though a flicker of crimson remains here and there along the stream, where blueberry branches hold onto a few final leaves. In the colder water, red flames have intensified in white-edged fins, and scarlet has flared along the flanks of males, as mature brook trout have come into their spawning colors.

But what I see are gray and ghostlike fish, in gray-white instants against dark stone. They move like bullets in the water. These young-of-the-year brook trout are some of the few survivors of the legions of fry who worked their way out of streambed gravel far back in the year. It is clear that speed has been an asset in their living through three seasons. It is also evident that they have reached the cryptozooic stage at which being seen is equated with the end of existence. Propelled by a terror of open water, even here in the dusky, dimly lit backwaters, they streak into new hiding spaces as I shift some of the rocks in their stream. They are loath to enter the deeper, open central current of the brook. These three- to four-inch trout sense a greater danger out there than the menace represented by my shadow-shape moving above the shallows. They are bronzy silver and blackened smudge, with speckles of light scattered all over their parr marks, well suited to the shadows and sand-glitter in the stream. Their adornments are too small, and the light too far gone in the water, for me to detect any gold or crimson along their flashing sides. Are there four fish or are there seven? It could almost be one, here and there and everywhere all at the same time.

Even in their panic they possess a fluid grace. These young-of-the-year have achieved some size and begun to develop a knowledge of their waterway. These attributes and the blending of trout intelligence and instinct that kept them alive as scores and scores of their year-class came to the end of their brief lives will be tested by the winter they are soon to enter. Pressed by their nature to grow quickly and become strong, these fish could have been seen in early spring, as they avoided cover and foraged ceaselessly. But by the time they had grown to a length of an inch and a half or so and entered their first summer, they had become furtive swimmers of tangle-strewn edgewaters and shadow-laced stone-spaces. Size, a paramount factor in the lives of salmonids, is a critical consideration even in these fingerlings, where an extra sixteenth of an inch in length might designate or determine a dominant trout. At one inch, some brook trout aggressively defend feeding stations, remaining ever-vigilant as they forage, and excluding other young-of-the-year from their preferred places. At the same time, they keep out of the feeding stations of older-age classes, and avoid the depths in which larger trout might prey on them. Danger comes not only by way of water; these first-year fish must constantly watch for the birds and mammals who stalk the shallows. Facing into the current, that source to which trout keep their heads turned all their lives, these tiny ones, like the adults they may become, are poised to forage, defend their feeding stations, or flee.

Territorial ones will vigorously drive away any who come within four or five body lengths, especially in the upstream source of drift. As they increase in length, they proportionally extend the area of the territory they defend, but it is always measured against the zone on the surface, in the water column, or on the bottom, in which they feed. The demanding bioenergetics of life in flowing water place sharply defined limits on activity, and a trout cannot exhaust himself in maintaining a territory beyond the one that meets his needs.

I wish these darting young-of-the-year would hold still for a moment. For some time I have been on my knees among them, in the most transparent water, and still cannot claim to have seen any of them clearly. One is never allowed more than a glimpse of these wild fish, it seems. Even on a line, as long as life is left in them, they are so elusive that even eyes cannot catch and hold them. A fine-meshed net would not help me here, these trout are so quick and skillful among the stones. How many trout would we taste, if we had only our hands with which to catch them? Chill, late-October water runs off my boots as I rise and wade on out the stream, traveling with its current. I'll see no more of trout, until I climb the bank at my leaving-

place. There is cricket-song and water-murmur as I look down on the twilight-silvered stream. The sun has settled out of sight to the west, the day-ending light becomes a hazy glow. All the slender brookside stems and branches are perfect black reflections on the still, glassy backwaters. Stirred by inlets and meanders over broken dams of collected leaves, the main channel shimmers. The white and silver water, with its fine black lines and inky shapes, becomes more sharply defined as landforms blur. A fish—perhaps a trout—noses the surface below my lookout. They can move anywhere now in the autumn-cooled waters, their brilliant red spots tiny accents turning black as evening moves into the water.

Study of a native brook trout

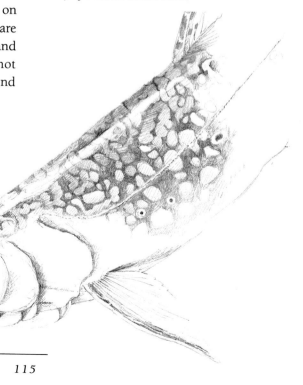

115

On this mild, late-autumn day, I take a long walk up Blackwater Brook to search for pools where trout are likely to have begun their courtship rituals. Some of the trout of this brook pair off in sand- and gravel-bottomed pools and riffles among the lowland alder runs, where the autumn-through-spring flow of current creates constant upwellings and prevents any debris from settling. Brook trout require upward-moving circulation through their redds, rather than the direct, rushing flow through nesting sites sufficient for most salmonid spawning. Unlike other stream species, brook trout are able to spawn in ponds and lakes where areas of upwelling groundwater are available to them, and they have a remarkable capacity for detecting such sources even in streams and ponds in which the water temperature is exactly the same as that of the groundwater bubbling up through the substrate. If there were no reaches of gravel with such circulation available along this brook, it would not be able to support a population of native brook trout. But they find spawning sites here and there, pairing off in turbulent runs only a few feet in length and only ten inches or so deep.

A short way up a stretch of riffles I glimpse trout-rushes in the water. Dark shapes dart at one another in swift pursuits and sudden separations. In the ever-changing theater of the water I cannot clearly discern the players, or even count them. They appear and disappear, and no one of them holds the stage for long. A single trout can at times appear to be several, in rippling swirls and staccatoes of flickering lights on the surface, and can at other times hide himself completely in nothing more than broken water. I make a slow approach, weave myself in among the dense lower branches of a streamside hemlock, and look down into the brook. The golden sand bottom, with its settings of black stones, is scattered with rosettes of watercress, evergreen and bright in the water. I see one trout drive another off, and then vanish. I had not even noticed the one who was chased away, until he took flight. Now I see a female holding her place in the flowing water. She materializes against a string of black stones studding the gravel at the bottom of the swiftest current. Slowly, she advances. For a moment I have the clearest view of her head. Her speckled side seems long in the water, and the white edges of her fins are dramatic. She slips ahead into turbulent water that erases any trace of her image. She reappears (or it is another?) in motionless suspension over gravel. It seems she has chosen this place to cut her redd. A male floats out of the current and hovers at her side; at least I think I have the male and female sorted out correctly. Yes, he is soon off in the direction of a fleeing fish shape, driving away a less than resolute challenge from another male.

Females, males, however they may be aligned at any one moment, both sexes are here, and the intricate courtship of the brook trout has begun. Once again the hierarchy of trout in a stream comes into play: it is the largest male who occupies the pool with the nest-building female. But unlike the quickly resolved disputes involving a territorial position with a favored feeding lane and cover, the order never seems to hold or go uncontested throughout the prolonged spawning season, as challengers continually invade the pool and the dominant male is constantly occupied with driving them off. These males are brilliant, even by the already stunning standards of native brook trout. I can easily see the infusion of color, like flames in the water, the intense purply red of tails and fins, and the scarlet red glowing along the flanks. The most form-destroying ripples and braids cannot wash away this blaze, an intensified flush that comes into the everyday splendor of the males several weeks in advance of the mid-October to early November spawning season. At this time they develop a hook in their lower jaw, the kype, which sprouts strong new teeth to back up the messages of their emboldened coloration, flarings of fins, and open-mouthed threats. (The kype of the male brook trout does not attain the exaggerated form and dimension that it does in other salmonids.) Show, and specifically size, usually settles confrontations, but dominant males defending their place alongside a female are not reluctant to sink their teeth into challengers who do not respond to subtler warnings.

Three smaller males are lined up in a shallow pool a short distance downstream. Each time the dominant trout of this stretch races upstream to drive off his principal rival, one or two of the smaller males dash up into the pool and take a place at the female's side. The moment the larger male charges back to reclaim his intended mate, these young bucks jet downstream, wheel sharply in abrupt about-faces, and once again take up their holding patterns. As he makes a brisk, triumphant tour of his cleared-out pool, the larger male tilts into the low sunlight just now beginning to leave the brook, and truly catches fire in the water. With no adversaries to face for a moment, he circles to the female's side, where he appears a reddish coppery-brown alongside her more pale, olive-green coloration. Females do not take on the pronounced red flush or intensified brilliance of the males, but her fins glow red, and her tail, though not so fiery as that of her suitor, is a deep, ruby-red purple. The slashes of sharpest white on the leading edges of the fins of all of these fish are absolutely striking, even beneath broken water. The backs of the younger males look gray-green and ghostlike against blackish, pulsing masses of fountain moss in the lower pools.

The female drifts back with the current, and rolls over on her side, flashing her white belly to the sun in the clear water. In the tail of the pool, gold waverings are like a netting of sunlight, which is broken up in the silver rushing of water into the riffles immediately below. Her whole body shudders as she whips her tail against the bottom, raising a fine dust of sand and tiniest gravel that glitters in midwater as it settles back to the substrate below the redd she is

clearing. The male continues attendant upon her every move, echoing, counterpoising, in what looks like a blend of ritualistic, patterned choreography and pure improvisation, a water ballet as fluid as the medium in which it is staged. The male's tail flares fully, he nudges and noses the female, as though prompting her to action. Then he bucks like a horse, mouth open, gills distended, bent sharply along his spine, head-up, all fins spread to their full width, and stiffened. Above the rippled gurgling of the brook I hear a startling break of water, and look quickly downstream just in time to see a trout shoot himself sideways up and over a spillway about twelve feet downstream of the courting couple. This acrobatic one streaks upstream, scattering the waiting line of younger, hopeful males who continue to hold in place, and enters the spawning arena. This newcomer is good-sized, and he tries to enhance his stature by elevating his head and raising his dorsal fin full-flag, but he is not the equal of the one he would unseat. Nevertheless, he puts up a spirited effort, alternately darting into the face of and swiftly fleeing from the defending male, their wild chase circling the developing redd, and careening all over the spawning run. The larger male appears confident in his every slashing movement, but he is put through some strenuous paces over an area comprising three flowing pools as he attempts to drive away the intruder once and for all. While he is thus diverted, a sec-

ond interloper moves up from among the downstream waiting males, taking a short-lived advantage to be at the female's side. The dominant male manages to drive him off even as he continues the conflict with his more serious contender, whom he must oppose with something more forceful than display and posturing. Throughout this several-minute disputation he must frequently break off his main contest to drive away the oportunistic young suitors. His determination and unflagging vigor serve him well; at length order is restored, and customary trout hierarchy holds for a time. In the icy water the speed of this brilliant fish, who by all appearances will be father to quite a number of potential natives for this brook, is breathtaking, as are his gyrations in combat. In his sudden stops he brakes himself in part with a sharp lateral twist of his dorsal fin, so that it is perpendicular to his streamlined body. I suspect that the alternate flarings and compressions of these fishes' fins, especially the dorsal fin, are a series of communications well understood in the trout's world.

Throughout the aggressive encounters of the combatant males, the female has continued periodic sweepings of the gravel, with strong thrusts of her body and tail. I have seen no other female in my surveillance area, and assume this one has herself cleared away any others from the place in which she intends to nest. She may have already completed some of her nesting and,

Trout ascending a waterfall

Caddis fly

if so, will be a battler herself as she defends committed eggs against intruding males who would mix eating previously released eggs with attempts to fertilize her subsequent releases. For the present, the courtship pair has the pool and its associated riffles all to themselves. With one pectoral fin thrust ahead and the other at his side, the male twists his body and vibrates his tail, hovering in the turbulent current much as a sparrowhawk gyrates to hold a stationary place in the wild, buffeting winds of March. He then moves to the female's side when she rights herself after her sinuous thrustings and twistings to excavate and clean the redd. They seem to brush sides, and at times their pectoral fins cross. She wheels off again, turning on her side and beating her tail wildly against the substrate. The male again hovers in place. In brook trout, the male does not take part in nest-building. Shadows overtake the pool, fish-shapes are harder to discern. The afternoon cools. A mating pair of caddis flies alights on my thumb, the near-triangular wings of one clasped over those of the other along the rear margins, forming a sort of discreet tent in which I assume their bodies unite, with their heads facing in opposite directions. It seems all out of season to be in the midst of mating rituals in leafless November. The caddis flies might have been inspired by the past two days, gifts of great mildness, which the month annually seems to offer briefly amid shivering intimations of winter. These insects have appeared all over and along the brook as I have watched the trout. I have seen several of the waiting males rise to take caddis flies entrapped and adrift on the currrent. The courting trout know nothing of the mild afternoon above the brook. The water is 48°F, about the midpoint of the customary spawning range of 40°F to 55°F. The brook is cold and clear; it has been running freely through the shortening days and lengthening nights, and its own internal weather will change only in growing colder and, eventually, in being closed over by unmoving clouds of ice and snow.

The male and female rise and fall in the water, circle and hover, weave around each other in the same watery space. I have never seen fish more fluid. At times they shimmy off to the side, in a sort of sideways walk out of the current, to rest in still edgewaters. The female becomes very active again, and works in the gravel with vigorous, belly-flashing turns and thrusts, her sleek body and cupped tail becoming tools for forcing water against a gritty matrix she herself does not touch, but moves and shapes by means of skillful hydraulics. She is truly digging now, creating an egg pocket in the shallow redd she has already excavated and cleared of all detritus and fine sand. She washes away any material that would impede a brisk circulation of water throughout the gravel spaces, a flow and upwelling critical for supplying oxygen during incubation, and for preventing the settling-in of sediments over the months that will pass before the fry are ready to depart their nest of tiny stones. She settles over the egg pit and arches downward drastically so that her anal fin can probe its depth. Her tail and back are sharply curved upward, her frozen position suggesting a seahorse. The male rushes in, but she is away and wheeling on her side again, working her tail strenuously.

She is typical of her species, which is more active and thorough in cutting a redd than any other trout. The male attends. Again she settles into her redd, curving her spine in a deep crook, thrusting her anal fin full length into the egg chamber she has fashioned. Her dorsal fin is erect and flaring; she ripples it wildly while opening her mouth in a wide gape. At once the male is at her side. He forms a close, shivering parallel to her rapidly quivering body, his own vibrating dorsal fin held high, his head arched abruptly upward and his large mouth distended remarkably. He shakes his head visibly and in a few shuddering seconds releases his milt simultaneously with her release of eggs. For a moment the cloud of milt is visible in the swirling water and around the shivering fish. Smaller males, two or three, too quick to count, make darting passes and take split-second holds near the mating pair. I cannot tell if they are releasing milt or attempting to steal a few of the eggs.

All the ritual, all the time and effort expended by the pair in their separate roles, culminates in this union that lasts a few, vibrant seconds. The male moves off immediately. He may go on to spawn with another female elsewhere along the brook, or he may have already spawned several times and be embarking on his solitary winter. The female remains. She crisscrosses her redd, with serpentine twists, in a slow, sinuous motion as she washes the fertilized eggs into spaces in the gravel and sweeps a clean cover of finer gravel over the egg pit. As they are with the cutting of their redds, female brook trout are considerably more thorough in covering it after spawning than are other trout species. This one may continue for another hour on this labor, finishing up by forcing larger stones over her spawning site. She may have already spawned with the same male. Over a period of several days a female brook trout may dig three or four pits, entrusting shares of eggs to each, until she is spent. This female, who appears to be about ten inches long, may lay as many as one thousand eggs this season. With such seemingly prolific numbers trout, like any other fish, endeavor to offset the extremely high mortality they face. If this spawning trout's complement is indeed a thousand

eggs by the time her nesting is completed, she may prove to be the mother of a half dozen brook trout from this year's class who live to ages two or three. One factor enabling native brook trout to live on in tiny, unfished streams is that a female as small as four inches, at the end of her second summer of growth, can produce nearly one hundred eggs.

With the exception of the spring-spawning rainbow trout, other salmonids in their natural ranges (and those species that have been shifted around as a result of fisheries management) are engaged in their nesting migrations and spawning rituals. The courtship and mating of brown trout are similar to that of brook trout. As one egg pit

*Lake trout (*Salvelinus namaycush*)*
spawning

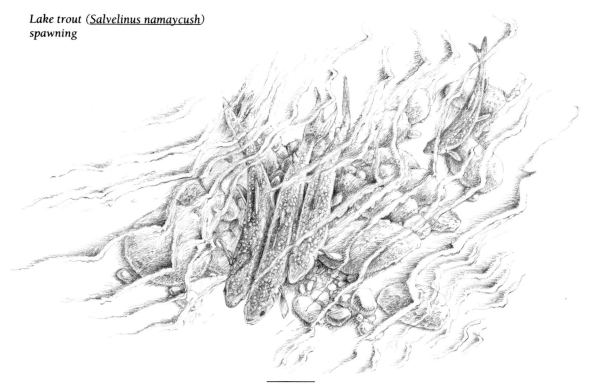

is completed, and the pair's simultaneous, shuddering release of milt and eggs is accomplished, the female advances just upstream and begins digging another egg pit. The gravel she dislodges is washed downstream to cover the fertilized eggs so recently left behind. Depending on their size, female brown trout lay from two hundred to six thousand eggs. Another fall spawner, but one of a nonstream habitat, and who breaks from some of the typical reproductive patterns of the salmonids, is the lake trout. The dark, cold, windswept nights of November's wintry spells bring the males to the breeding shoals of the deep lakes in which they live. They precede the females by several days, and often work to clear out spawning grounds, washing and scraping away detritus and algae from beds of one- to six-inch-diameter rocks, which will receive the eggs. Lake trout make no nests, nor is it their practice to form single pairs for spawning. Commonly, two males compress a female between them, and the trio of stiffened, shivering bodies release their eggs and milt in a mating climax of a few seconds. Several males and more than one female may be involved in the spawning act, during which fertilized eggs are scattered over the nesting bed, to settle among the crevices among the stones. There is no covering of the eggs. The mating groups mingle and interchange throughout spawning, which, in another departure from typical salmonid habits, takes place in the evening. The spawners depart the nesting grounds after the evening's mat-

ing, to reassemble after nightfall the next day, if conditions are right, and continue the spawning, which generally extends over a two-week period. These are trout of deep, dark water. Storms in the November nights seem to encourage their spawning, and mild, tranquil, moonlit nights will delay it. As with brook and brown trout, lake trout eggs develop over winter and hatch late in that season or early in spring. Spawning beds are usually selected on rock-strewn, wave-tossed shoals or reefs in one to four feet of water. The wind and waves here serve the aerating, cleansing function for lake trout that upwellings of water provide for brook trout. The variation that seems forever at work among the salmonids is evidenced by some subpopulations of lake trout in the Great Lakes. One of these, called the siscowet, spawns at depths approaching three hundred feet. The more customary habit of nesting in shallow water leaves lake trout eggs vulnerable to stranding by late-season drawdowns.

The brook trout I leave to the covering of her redd in Blackwater Brook will not have to worry about drawdowns, at least. She will move on, and select her overwintering place; her eggs will begin their winter-long incubation. Barring some extreme in the natural scheme of things along this waterway, such as an excessive flood or scouring of ice, her early November spawning will result in the emergence by next March of fingerlings who will be part of that year's brook trout class.

The Closing Over: Return to Silence

Nature's silence is its one remark...
—*Annie Dillard*

Royal Fern Pool: 20 November

On an upstream walk, from Willow Pool to Royal Fern Pool, I search the smaller water-holds and runs. The screens of alder, silky dogwood, winterberry holly, and willow are leafless, yet concealing. The innumerable twigs, branches, stems, and trunks obscure everything beyond the most immediate vision. Near at hand, the sun and my eyesight do find an access into the world of the trout. Through openings among branches low to the water, I can look deep into the

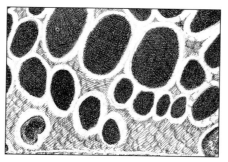

brook. The trout will keep close to shadows now. I steal quietly up to the large red maples and peer among their undermined but anchoring roots, as I have for many successive seasons. Trout come here. I know that, though I have yet to make a sighting. I lean against the trees and wait awhile, watching the late autumn water slide by. An occasional leaf drifts past, slowly turning end-over-end in the current, dark, burnt out by the season's passing and immersion in the brook. The larger trout of this waterway surely know of this cryptic undercut and its sheltering maples, but today, again, it seems they will remain hidden. Like the Willow Pool, this profound place remains a mystery to me.

Anticipation, and I suppose my alertness, grow as I approach the Royal Fern Pool. I have something of a picture to go by here, where I have sighted trout before. Perhaps my first sighting of a trout at Willow Pool or within the red maple undercut, whenever it may come, will lead to many subsequent ones; it seems I need to see a trout before I can see trout. The tail of Royal Fern Pool is only thirty yards or so upstream of the undercut; any trout familiar with one of these locations knows the other. It could be that the largest trout of this brook keep to these most occult places. A brook trout in the twelve-inch class would go undisputed in the best lies and holds of this entire stream, I would imagine. Maybe I have never yet approached these seemingly desirable niches quietly enough, or kept still long enough, to see the speckled fish they hold. As such musings entertain my mind, my eyes detect a faint cloud of stirred-up mud in a hollow against the base of the sloping bank, in the tail of the pool. It is not a fish, I am sure, but I watch for any revelation. There is not a movement as the mud-cloud dissipates. I probe the area lightly with the tip of my walking stick, discovering the round entrance of an underwater burrow, two feet or so below the surface. It is too small to be the doorway of a bank-lodge of the beavers who keep a major sluiceway open down the embankment only a few yards away, for the transportation of their cut trees and branches into the brook. I'm not sure where these extremely active beavers live just now, for all my surveillance of this brook. This burrow would more likely be the work of muskrats, though I'm not familiar with them along such wooded, shrub-enclosed stretches of water. I'd think they'd keep a lodging closer to their own dinner grounds, in the burreeds and other herbaceous growth choking the abandoned beaver pond above Willow Pool. I consider, very briefly, reaching into the tunnel to see if I can feel the shell of any wood turtle who might have retreated there for the winter; there are documentations of various turtle species hibernating in underwater muskrat burrows. But I am loath to reach bare-handed into animal tunnels on dry land, let alone those beneath the water…something about teeth, and some future uses I have in mind for my fingers.

My question is answered unequivocably as a muskrat explodes out of the hole and torpedoes upstream, covering the length of Royal Fern Pool and disappearing in an instant. I watch, but never see him surface. Either this one can hold his breath a good long while or he has made it to another bank tunnel, well known to him but not to me. So, I discover another resident of this ten-yard-wide, thirty-yard-long pool, which is so favored over various seasons by trout, blacknosed dace, white suckers, wood turtles, young green and bull frogs, caddis flies, crayfish, and beavers. I know it also to be on the main circuit of the minks' prowling, and frequently find its muddy banks impressed with tracks of raccoon and white-tailed deer at times of low water.

What I have come to call the Royal Fern Pool is a critical component of the brook's ecosystem. It does not exist, nor could it flourish, in isolation. This pool and others along this lower-gradient run, most of which are well concealed by shrubby canopies, shelter larger trout and other animals. Few water plants can grow beneath the dense overgrowth, and the primary source of nutrients of this reach of the brook is the leaf and twig debris that falls into its waters, becomes sodden, and sinks, to be entrapped by trailing branches, stones, and sunken logs, and held back by debris dams and beaver impoundments. Here the leaves, bits of bark, broken twigs, and other plant material are worked upon by insects and microorganisms that collect, shred, con-

sume, and recycle. From materials brought into the brook by wind and rain, leaf-fall, beavers, and muskrats, the stream receives the energy base upon which its animals live. Everything that slows the water, detains it for a time, or causes it to double back upon itself, allowing a settling of plant debris, or a straining of organic material from the passing current, sustains the brook's abundant invertebrate life. And this in turn sustains the trout. Each submersed twig that fingers a sodden leaf from the ever-flowing stream has a bearing on the trout who flash their white-edged fins in Royal Fern Pool. The severe and extensive loss of habitat to which trout have been subjected is exacerbated by every removal of a flow obstruction, every "neatening," straightening, or channelizing of a stream or river. It is not only the great dams blocking the mightiest rivers that have set back the salmonids so devastatingly.

Perhaps the spread of human activity is never so destructive as when it reaches the edge of a trout stream. Many still think, even after the destruction of over half the wetlands in the United States (an ongoing loss), that a major concession has been made to nature when a buffer of twenty-five feet of riparian zone is left along a stream; many others would consider that too much. We prefer our picnic tables at the water's edge to wild trout swimming in it. Wild places cannot be so bounded; the trout's world does not end at the edge of his brook.

Among alders so intertwined I must walk in a crouch, I move upstream, to the fern mound itself. The waist-high, ornamental sprays of royal fern are gone now, fallen and crumbled away to make their contribution to the water sliding by. I see that the beavers have taken down a young brookside elm that has grown here for a number of years. This cutting will result in a new opening in the brookside canopy next year, assisting the fern's luxuriant growth and providing extra sunning niches for the pool's resident frogs and wood turtles. The beavers have not taken this tree away. Their work at times seems to have a management intent separate from food or construction. Rhythms and behaviors in natural systems can defy human interpretation. For now, the ferns would appear to be favored, and the elm will have to start anew next spring from life sequestered in its roots. In neoprene waders, I brace my right knee in the shallow water of the submerged shelf between the fern mound and the banking, and extend my left leg into the brook, to a foothold on the sandy bottom in thirty inches or so of water. This position-taking startles a young green frog I had not noticed on a mossy hummock nearby.

Abandoning thoughts of trout for a moment, I decide to grope in under the fern mound, bank, and their associated tree roots and rocks, to see if I might feel the shell of a hibernating wood turtle. I feel nothing but the agonizing cold of the water, which is 12° below the already bone-chilling temperatures preferred by trout. My explorations are brief. After two immersions each, my arms and hands take on a mind of their own, and cannot be forced to enter the water. And to think the brook's temperature will continue its descent, until it is barely a degree above freezing. As I rub my arms and hands against my shirt and vest in an effort to dry them and alleviate the pain, I detect stirrings in the backwaters around the fern mound. Amid suspended leaves I spot the serrated rear edge of a young wood turtle's shell. I pull this little one out of the water for a moment, and recognize him as one I found here a year ago last April, a two-year-old just out of hibernation, basking in dry leaves among upreaching alder stems on the opposite bank of this pool. I saw him once again that year, in mid-October, ten or fifteen yards upstream of where I now kneel. He or she (too young to tell yet) was the last turtle I saw last year, and will probably share that distinction this year. I slip him back among the sunken leaves, and he tunnels, with surprising alacrity, out of sight. The water on this submarine shelf is only seven or eight inches deep, and will freeze solid as winter settles in. The little turtle will drop deeper into the pool before then. He knows where to spend the winter here.

I shift my eyes back to the depths at midstream, the glowing, clear-swept spread of sand and the current-washed bed of gravel just upstream of it. As though on cue, a trout drifts into view, emerging sideways from a covering of red branches. He is silhouetted sharply against the sand as he drops backward with the current and then fades sideways back beneath the obscuring branches. He reappears and hovers in the central flow, a few feet from my immersed leg. I have become a part of the brook now, apparently, and will be pleased to stay so, until physical limitations force me to move. The trout advances against the current and moves magically in the water, as though drawn by invisible strings. His design is so perfectly suited to the flowing of this dense medium of his life that he floats, ghostlike, at his own pace, with it, across it, or against it, with no apparent outward motion. As he moves up the pool, he slides to his right, toward the fern mound and its surrounding labyrinth of branches. Here he comes suddenly to the side of another, larger, trout. He parallels her. I see clearly enough now to discern them as a pair. The male curls away in the current, flashing the red along his flanks and in his fins, then turns to hover at her side once more. Abundant soft gold speckles glow out from her deep olive sides; her stabilizing fins are purple-red, with

white outer margins that stand out sharply even against the background of pale sand beneath her. She is large, a queen of this brook; her streamlined form, facing lance-straight into the current, appears a little over a foot long. Her attendant prince is on the order of ten inches, and likely a dominant force in this stream's trout hierarchy. They part, take courtly sweeps in opposite directions, and then rejoin to line up parallel with each other, noses to the flow. I would have thought spawning to be over by now, but these seasons of the wild trout have their extensions; in concert with their waters, their life-history parameters are not rigid. Their dance, however brief, seemed to have been about courting—they have an apparent interest in coming together, rather than driving the other away. I wait, anticipating their taking up a nesting ballet over the gravel bed immediately upstream. I have come to expect anything of this marvelous pool. Instead, they calmly turn beneath obscuring branches and disappear in the undercuts of the fern mound. I keep my place a while longer, but they do not reappear and this encounter with trout proves, as most do, a brief one. There is never enough of seeing these animals a-fin in the beautiful waters of their lives. I cannot keep still any longer in this cold water; one leg aches to straighten, the other to bend, and my curved back, even in the uncommonly warm November sun, complains painfully. I keep my eyes on the pool as I crawl back up onto the bank and stand up. There is no re-emergence of the amorous trout. They are

well aware of me now, and will keep to their tangles.

I move upstream, searching the head of this pool, then the riffles above it, and a second smaller pool above the riffles. The bottom has been swept almost completely clear here. But there are occasional sunken branches, partialy embedded in the sand, and these have collected modest accumulations of waterlogged leaves and twigs. Nosed into one such holdfast, on clear golden sand, rests a wintering wood turtle. Her carapace, though covered only along its front rim, where she has lodged herself into the branches, is easily lost in the collection of leaves surrounding her. Her shell, wedged in place, appears and disappears as I strive to look through the water's unraveling braids. Trusting this scant, though effective, concealment and the invulnerability of her shell, she rests motionless within her own bones. She may shift her position as winter deepens.

No trout could keep the winter where this turtle lies. There can be no sedentary, stonelike settling to the bottom, oblivious to the water streaming over; current-battling trout would become exhausted within minutes where it appears this turtle could lie for months. Although the cold water is well oxygenated, a fish's energy would be quickly depleted, with sugar reserves spent and lethal levels of lactic acid built up. Trout tire easily; lactic acid accumulates much more rapidly in their tissues even than in those of mammals, and trout require six to twelve times as long to get rid

of it. This accounts for their habit of moving swiftly in short bursts, and resting often. This factor must be taken into account in playing a trout who is intended for release. As adept as they are in the medium of swirling streams, trout require quiet waters. In winter, restorative lulls, out of the way of the constant flowing, are especially important to salmonids. The wood turtle will not eat, and likely will not breathe again in open air until late March or early April. A possible slight uptake of oxygen from the water through her skin or throat lining may be her only access to oxygen for months. The trout will never cease working their mouths and gills in the icy water as they extract the oxygen essential for metabolism, however comparatively subdued it may become. Most of them will probably feed, although in water a degree or two above freezing trout can survive upwards of four months without eating. They will withdraw to hidden stillwater places in the tumultuous winter stream, to the water within water where one leaf can rest upon another without the slightest stirring, while inches away the current races by, in a rush to a river miles downstream.

In the dense shade of the one white pine tree among the brookside alders, there are glitterings of ice, delicate spikes, fleurs-de-lis, thin, intricate shelvings. A deer's breathing could melt them. But low to the earth that has begun to freeze along the chilling brook, and sheltered by the cold-embracing shadow of the pine, these first featherings of the ice that will, in time, encase the entire brook, persist. On such fragile footings, bridges will be built and, eventually, spans that deer can walk. The turtle may shift in the stream, the trout may hover for weeks beneath weavings of maroon-red branches; but I will be shut out from looking in on their world.

Sleet and Rain: 26 November

In last daylight sleet begins to rattle down among bare branches and rustle on the leaf-strewn bank; not precipitation running along stems and trunks to drip and soften on leaves or sink into moss, but precipitation that strikes sharply against and bounces off any surface it encounters on its journey from the clouds. This wild sound in growing November darkness brings back memories of my first walks along wild brooks. Something speaks of my own personal origins in this light at this time of year, and the stillness of this day, as though my very first encounter with earth and water came at such a moment. I remember these things clearly: the silver of the brook threading off to invisibility in the merging of earth and sky and branches in gathering darkness, the stunning, exciting silence and aloneness. I think back over four decades to find the first such times. Over the course of my life I have had to move steadily north, to retreat, withdraw northward, to find these times and places, to keep these moments. I could not have imagined, when I was just a boy, and my heart was bonding with wooded brooks and open swamps, how far I would have to

travel, what a journey would be required, to keep to the streams, to be able to stand at twilight, alone on the bank of a murmuring pool, in which wood turtles sleep and trout abide.

The wintry scent of sleet yields to a momentary springlike earth-smell, as sleet turns into rain. I sift the scents and no, it is not March mud I smell, but November earth; not a streambank on the edge of thaw, but a streambank on the verge of freeze. The pebbling sound of sleet on water changes to the whispering sound of rain on water, and mingles with the brook's own water-sounds. There seems a recognition, a familiarity in this, a brotherhood or sisterhood in the dialogue of sleet and rain and brook. Darkness deepens and, among the other magic that it works, turns rain back into sleet. I remember anew that exhilarating, primal solitude and silence, that encompassing quiet with its small, sporadic sounds, such as the water's intermittent whisper and the widely spaced one- or two-note calls from unseen birds. I never wanted the silence and its small sounds to be lost to me. I find them here now, in sleet and rain, on the bank of another silver brook glimmering away out of sight on the edge of nightfall.

December Trout: 1 December

An afternoon walk up Willow Brook. The lowering, pre-solstice sun reaches into this section of the brook, a sparkling lane of water cutting through a woods of leafless

The brook arranges things

trees, at an illuminating angle. I often time my walks with the sun; there are morning brooks and afternoon brooks, and morning and afternoon sides of brooks. I adjust my hours with the seasons to establish times at which I return again and again to favorite runs of water. The sun and the cycling of the seasons are my chronometer. Here the water has a steady, quiet slide; how beautifully, how easily it divides and comes back together again.

The brook arranges things, sorts and files and keeps them for a time. Autumn leaves are collected against boulders, in the order of their falling, sticks are sorted and stacked, or laid side by side. Masses of fallen leaves are separated from twigs and grasses and swept into compact drifts in pockets and backwaters, sometimes filed edgewise, sometimes stacked in flat layers. Small stones are graded, coarse, medium, and fine, as is sand; all are sorted by size and texture, put in place, and held in place for a time.

Cornered by the stone on which I stand, and left carefully in place on a gravel bar, lies a mat of pine needles, grasses, twigs, and bits of larger branches. The pattern in their weaving still traces the movement of the current that wove it, as though water had been transformed into a fiber tapestry. Not a hair out of place, it seems. This bark cloth has a lacelike border of ten-

133

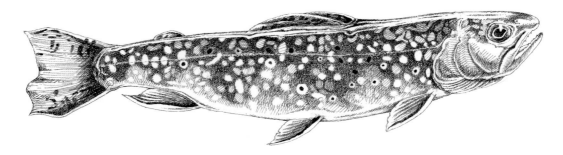

tative ice that will in time advance and set this pattern for a season. This drift of leaves, pine needles, straw, and twigs will hold until the restless flows of late-winter spates and spring thaw set the brook to rearranging.

I come to one of my watching-places, where I can wedge myself in among the five sturdy trunks of a red maple sprout-clump reaching up from the outer margin of the bank. Close-grown clusters of trees or sturdier shrubs arching out over streams and rivers invite this kind of wedging-in, and waiting and watching. Somewhat like the kingfishers, I have my perches, though my feet are rarely more than a foot above the earth, and I have yet to dive for a fish. A brook trout, beautiful *Salvelinus fontinalis,* swims by below me, with the current, down the center of this open run of Willow Brook. This handsome brook char, wonderful "little salmon of the cold springs," seems on a mission, if not a migration. With slow, snakelike undulations from side to side and a steadily swishing tail, the speckled fish cruises with the water's flow, altering neither pace nor course, and is out of sight in a matter of seconds. He seemed in midjourney, as though he had come a ways in just this fash-

ion, and had a ways to go. This trout may be a holdover, a stocked fish who defied the staggering odds and survived not only fishing season but also natural predation. No anglers have cast to this brook for months, I'd guess, but the mink have never ceased their patrolling, and the kingfishers will keep an eye out as long as there is open water. The brook trout was profusely speckled; a rich display of pale spots of all sizes stood out against a rich green background. The white fin-edges were characteristically readable in the water, even though the fins were compressed. I detected no red. Still, this could have been a native, a female; perhaps even a male in whom the spawning colors have quieted some, as the brook and the year itself have begun to quiet. The trout's journey appeared purposeful enough, although the water is about 35°F, far below the 61°F range best suited for sustained swimming by trout. But this was no steelhead on a thousand-mile spawning migration. This was a brook trout possibly shifting in the brook a bit, in preparation for the coming of the ice. The still water of the meadow pond above the upstream tributary of this brook section has already been closed over. There is a deep, brimful, two-year-old beaver pond about one hundred yards downstream, where featherings of ice have just begun along the shores. The trout who traveled by me may winter in that pond.

The sky this afternoon, following sunset, had a pale but radiant yellow glow, softening into a pink flush that went lavender before diffusing in the early darkening sky, suggestive of a rainbow trout. Several days ago, at about the same time, there was another trout-belly sky, with similar colors, but more of a solar-flare intensity; very much a brook-trout evening sky, with trees and branches jet black against it. Twilights around the time of winter solstice often suggest salmon, trout, and char.

Winter Solstice: 22 December

Uncommonly warm, haze- and fog enshrouded day at winter solstice. There is mist all along the brook; it is a mild and quiet, closed-in world. Hemlocks and white pines are brush paintings on the silk ground of the mist. In the hazy half-light of the stream, trout are brush paintings that come to life from time to time. Winter begins. This harsh season starts out with a compensating promise, a holding-in-place that ends the steady loss of daylight. This day marks a time that is at once an enduring and an advance. There is no turning back. Marking this turning on a point in time, space, and light, in clear water under ice, trout are waiting.

Kingfisher in Winter: 27 December

The startling call of a kingfisher rattles out of the silence of the snow-draped hemlocks. For a split second that familiar call, which I have not heard for months, disorients my place in the seasons. It feels as though I should stand in midsummer, but the sifting of snow against my face as I look up to search bare branches for the fish-hunting bird brings me quickly back to the end of December. I see only the gray maze of branches against dark pines, and the steady fall of snow on a windless day. A second call announces his appearance, with a flight that seems to stagger in the snow-filled air, as the kingfisher wings over an open stretch of water, his gray-blue head quite striking against the steely grays of winter. He sweeps up to take a perch on a dead overhang. Snow begins to settle on his shoulders and his crest as he peers into the black water below. He is soon off again, with a snow-shedding leap from his fishing-branch, and fades away in falling flakes, this time in silence. I am not likely to hear such a warm-season sound again until red-winged blackbirds retake the budding alders late next March. The kingfisher will stay this winter, as do some males of his kind, as long as there is open water to fish. The ice may yet drive him to the south, but he is one who will abandon a hard-won territory only grudgingly. Should he endure through winter, he will have the upper hand in keeping his fishing grounds and a nesting-burrow site to himself next spring, driving away any

challengers who arrive from their retreats to the south. Some memory of a wing-beating, bill-clashing fight last season provides him the resolution to keep to this watery avenue in the hemlocks, and try to outlast hunger and cold.

Trout could be wintering back under the ice-edge the kingfisher stared at so intently, if briefly. During this time of freezing water it is more important for these fish to find cover and conserve energy than it is for them to feed. Their metabolism slows, and heart rates that could reach one hundred beats per minute in 59°F water will drop as low as fifteen beats per minute in a 41°F brook. They abandon the stations they defended last spring and held all summer in favor of sanctuaries where they will be able to survive winter. In many cases, they have taken up overwintering holds collectively. Although they can be ferociously possessive and combatant about their warm-season feeding stations and holding lies, trout set aside their aggressive behavior as water temperatures decrease at the onset of winter, and come together in aggregates that will share space restricted by the vicissitudes of the cold season. Even in the most undisturbed and varied waterways there are only so many critical overwintering niches available, and trout must share them. Ice encroachment, lowering water levels, or the chutes and rapids of winter floods can force even greater numbers together and bring these generally solitary fish as close to a

Beaver dam in December

schooling behavior as they come in wild streams. This behavior may protect trout, as it does schooling species, by making it more difficult for a predator to target an individual in the shimmering confusion of the many. But it can also increase winter mortality, as such aggregates within severely restricted habitat can suffer heavy losses to such skillful underwater predators as mergansers and river otters. In a sense, schooled trout are like white-tailed deer yarded up in deep-drifted snow.

In situations where non-natives have been introduced, aggregations of overwintering trout may include more than one species. Many fishes resident in a given stream have the same primary requisites for wintering niches as do trout, but the evolution of different behaviors among them has made coexistence possible. Smaller sculpins, suckers, minnows, and other nonsalmonids withdraw from the main flow and take their places close to or in the substrate, in branch tangles and beneath stones and gravel, where they do not compete with trout for space. Larger nonsalmonids, such as fallfish and creek chubsuckers, journey to the deepest pools in the stream system and spend the winter there, migrating back upstream as water warms in spring. Among the trout, different age groups select varied shelters, helping to avoid conflict and possible cannibalism. Young fish often take to the smallest tributaries, which exclude the entrance of the largest adults.

Black tumbles of water murmur themselves out of sight and sound beneath

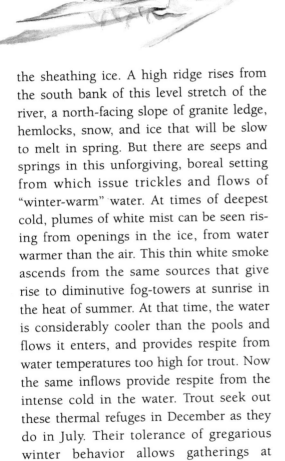

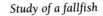

the sheathing ice. A high ridge rises from the south bank of this level stretch of the river, a north-facing slope of granite ledge, hemlocks, snow, and ice that will be slow to melt in spring. But there are seeps and springs in this unforgiving, boreal setting from which issue trickles and flows of "winter-warm" water. At times of deepest cold, plumes of white mist can be seen rising from openings in the ice, from water warmer than the air. This thin white smoke ascends from the same sources that give rise to diminutive fog-towers at sunrise in the heat of summer. At that time, the water is considerably cooler than the pools and flows it enters, and provides respite from water temperatures too high for trout. Now the same inflows provide respite from the intense cold in the water. Trout seek out these thermal refuges in December as they do in July. Their tolerance of gregarious winter behavior allows gatherings at sources of groundwater upwellings or inflows, and at the mouths of spring-fed tributaries. Inlets such as these offer stable flow, moderate temperatures, and enough

insect drift to meet their greatly reduced feeding requirements. In finding and sharing such refuges, congregations of trout seem to take on a single mind, and the aggregation behaves at times as though it were an individual fish. Under waterlogged lengths of trees that seasons ago fell into the stream, among jumbles of stones and branches, tails sweeping in unison, the fiercely independent trout of milder times are brought together in a forced brotherhood of endurance.

The Last Day of the Year: 31 December

During the course of cold days with thin sun, and long nights of deep cold under brilliant stars, ice closes up the water, gradually working outward from the shallow arc of the beaver dam, fingering over the uneven terrain along the shore, crystallizing across the surface to openings of deep water. Already the ice has extended in a silver sheet over the sphagnum shallows and become a solid plane in the beaver channel, holding tufts of rushes and sedges in place at the surface. Winter will advance until even the cascading waterfalls on high ridges are set in place, crystal staircases, ice-blue, ice-green, rising up the bouldered slopes.

Black water slips from beneath the forming ice, down through hidden spillways

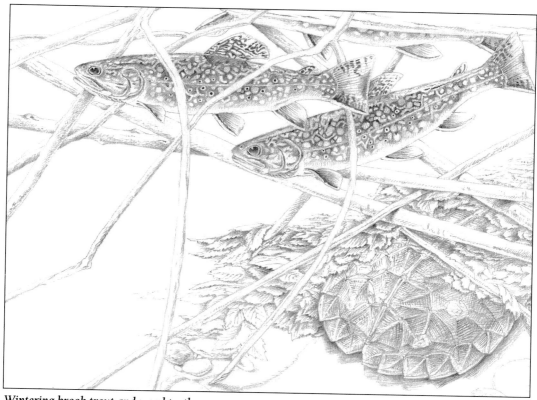

Wintering brook trout and wood turtle

within the beaver dam to run among the red maples and alders in a brook edged with emerald moss. The rippling, whispering current keeps itself free at the turning of the year, but soon it, too, will be closed over and silenced as the water is stilled, caught in place, arrested in motion by the deepening cold. For a time, until the first open water, I will be divided from the trout, yet linked with them in the waiting.

BIBLIOGRAPHY

Arbona, F. L. 1980. *Mayflies, the Angler, and the Trout.* Piscataway, N.J.: New Century Press.

Bachman, R. A. 1991. "Brown Trout." In *Trout,* edited by J. Stolz and J. Schnell, 208–228. Harrisburg, Pa.: Stackpole Books.

Barnhart, R. A. 1989. Symposium Review: Catch-and-Release Fishing, a Decade of Experience. *North American Journal of Fisheries Management* 9(1): 74–80.

Behnke, R. J. 1991. America's Changing Fish Fauna. *Trout.* Spring: 35–38.

Bergman, R. 1976. *Trout.* New York: Alfred A. Knopf.

Butler, R. L. 1991. "View From an Observation Tank." In *Trout,* edited by J. Stolz and J. Schnell. 50–56. Harrisburg, Pa.: Stackpole Books.

Cunjak, R. A., and J. M. Green. 1983. Habitat Utilization by Brook Char (*Salvelinus fontinalis*) and Rainbow Trout (*Salmo gairdneri*) in Newfoundland Streams. *Canadian Journal of Zoology* 61:1214–1219.

Cunjak, R. A., and G. Power 1986. Winter Habitat Utilization by Stream-Resident Brook Trout (*Salvelinus fontinalis*) and Brown Trout (*Salmo trutta*). *Canadian Journal of Fisheries and Aquatic Sciences* 43:1970–1981.

———. 1987. The Feeding and Energetics of Stream-Resident Trout in Winter. *Journal of Fish Biology* 31:493–511.

Fausch, K. D., and R. J. White 1981. Competition Between Brook Trout (*Salvelinus fontinalis*) and Brown Trout (*Salmo trutta*) for Positions in a Michigan Stream. *Canadian Journal of Fisheries and Aquatic Sciences* 38: 1220–1227.

Fausch, K. D. 1988. Tests of Competition Between Native and Introduced Salmonids in Streams: What Have We Learned? *Canadian Journal of Fisheries and Aquatic Sciences* 45: 2238–2246.

Flick, W. A., and D. A. Webster. 1964. Comparative First Year Survival and Production in Wild and Domestic Strains of Brook Trout *Salvelinus fontinalis*. *Transactions of the American Fisheries Society* 93:58–69.

Flick, W. A. 1991. "Brook Trout." In *Trout* edited by J. Stolz and J. Schnell, 196–207. Harrisburg, Pa: Stackpole Books.

Goodman, B. 1991. Keeping Anglers Happy Has a Price. *Bioscience* 41(5): 294–295.

Grant, J. W. A., and D. L. G. Noakes. 1987. Escape Behavior and Use of Cover by Young-of-the-Year Brook Trout *Salvelinus fontinalis*. *Canadian Journal of Fisheries and Aquatic Sciences* 44:1390–1396.

Grant, J. W. A., A. Grant, D. L. G. Noakes and K. M. Jones. 1989. Spatial Distribution of Defense and Foraging in Young-of-the-Year Brook Charr *Salvelinus fontinalis*. *The Journal of Animal Ecology* 58:773–784.

Griffith, J. S. 1974. Utilization of Invertebrate Drift by Brook Trout (*Salvelinus fontinalis*) and Cutthroat Trout (*S. clarki*) in Small Streams in Idaho. *Transactions of the American Fisheries Society* 103:440–447.

Heacox, C. E. 1974. *The Compleat Brown Trout*. New York: Winchester Press.

Hewitt, E. R. 1948. *A Trout and Salmon Fisherman for Seventy-Five Years*. New York: Charles Scribner's Sons.

Holland, D. 1949. *The Trout Fisherman's Bible*. New York: Doubleday and Company.

LaFontaine, G. 1981 *Caddisflies*. New York: Nick Lyons Books.

Langan, D., J. Braico and J. Spissinger. 1991. New York's Heritage Strain Brook Trout. New York State Department of Environmental Conservation: *The Conservationist* 45(5):32–33 .

Larson, G. L., and S. E. Moore. 1985. Encroachment of Exotic Rainbow Trout in the Southern Appalachian Mountains. *Transactions of the American Fisheries Society* 114:195–203.

Leiser, E. and R. H. Boyle. 1982. *Stoneflies for the Angler*. New York: Alfred A. Knopf.

Martin, N. V. 1951. A Study of the Lake Trout, *Salvelinus namaycush*, in Two Algonquin Park, Ontario, Lakes. *Transactions of the American Fisheries Society*. 81:111–137.

Mason, J. W., O. M. Brynildson and P. E. Degurse. 1967. Comparative Survival of Wild and Domestic Strains of Brook Trout in Streams. *Transactions of the American Fisheries Society* 96:313–319.

McFadden, J. T. 1961. *A Population Study of the Brook Trout, Salvelinus fontinalis.* No. 7. Bethesda, Md.: Wildlife Society.

McNichol, R. E., E. Scherer and E. J. Murkin. 1985. Quantitative Field Investigations of Feeding and Territorial Behavior of Young-of-the-Year Brook Charr, *Salvelinus fontinalis. Environmental Biology of the Fishes* 12(3): 219–229.

Moore, K. M. S. and S. V. Gregory. 1988. Response of Young-of-the-Year Cutthroat Trout to Manipulation of Habitat Structure in a Small Stream. *Transactions of the American Fisheries Society* 117:162–170.

Morgan, A. H. 1930. *Field Book of Ponds and Streams.* New York: G. P. Putnam and Sons.

Nilsson, N. A. and T.G. Northcote. 1981. Rainbow Trout (*Salmo gairdneri*) and Cutthroat Trout (*S. clarki*) Interactions in Coastal British Columbia Lakes. *Canadian Journal of Fisheries and Aquatic Sciences* 38:1228–1246.

Rhead, L. 1920. *Fisherman's Lures and Game-Fish Food.* New York: Charles Scribner's Sons.

Rosenbauer, T. 1988. *Reading Trout Streams.* New York: Nick Lyons Books.

Scarola, J. F. 1973. *Freshwater Fishes of New Hampshire.* Concord, N.H.: New Hampshire Department of Fish and Game.

Schwiebert, E. 1978. *Trout. Vols. 1 & 2.* New York: E. P. Dutton.

Stolz, J., and J. Schnell, eds. 1991. *Trout.* Harrisburg, Pa.: Stackpole Books.

Trench, C. C. 1974. *A History of Angling.* Chicago: Follett Publishing Company.

Ultsch, G. R. 1989. Ecology and Physiology of Hibernation and Overwintering Among Freshwater Fishes, Turtles and Snakes. *Biological Review* 64:435–516.

Vannote, R. L., G. W. Minshaw, K. W. Cummins, J. R. Sedell and C. E. Cushing. 1980. The River Continuum Concept. *Canadian Journal of Fisheries and Aquatic Sciences* 37:130–137.

Van Offelen, H. K. 1990. *Comparison of Performance and Behavior Characteristics Between Two Strains of Age 0 Brook Trout Stacked Into Adirondack Waters.* Master's Thesis, Cornell University, Ithaca, N.Y.

Waters, T. F. 1983. Replacement of Brook Trout by Brown Trout Over 15 Years in a Minnesota Stream: Production and Abundance. *Transactions of the American Fisheries Society* 112(2A):137–146.

Webster, D. A., and G. Eriksdottir. 1976. Upwelling Water as a Factor Influencing Spawning Sites by Brook Trout (*Salvelinus fontinalis*). *Transactions of the American Fisheries Society* 105:416–421.

Whitlock, D. 1982. *Guide to Aquatic Trout Foods.* New York: Nick Lyons Books.